1982

COMMUNITY DEVELOPMENT
RESEARCH

COMMUNITY DEVELOPMENT RESEARCH

Concepts, Issues, and Strategies

Edited by

Edward J. Blakely

University of California, Davis

HUMAN SCIENCES PRESS
72 Fifth Avenue   3 Henrietta Street
NEW YORK, NY 10011 ● LONDON, WC2E 8LU

Library of Congress Catalog Number 78-11568

ISBN: 0-87705-334-0
       0-87705-348-0

Copyright © 1979 by Human Sciences Press
72 Fifth Avenue, New York, New York 10011

Printed in the United States of America
9 987654321

Library of Congress Cataloging in Publication Data

Main entry under title:

Community development research.

    Includes index.
    1. Community development—United States—Addresses, essays, lectures. 2. Community development—Addresses, essays, lectures. 3. Social science research—Addresses Addresses, essays, lectures. I. Blakely, Edward James, 1938–
HN90.C6C662   301.34'07'2073   78-11568
ISBN 0-87705-334-0
    0-87705-348-0

CONTENTS

CONTRIBUTORS

Edward J. Blakely is Assistant Vice President, Academic Personnel Systemwide, University of California. Prior to assuming this post in 1977, Dr. Blakely was Associate Dean of Applied Economics and Behavioral Sciences and Assistant Director for Community Resource Development of the Cooperative Extension of the University of California, Davis. He is on the Board of Directors of the Community Development Society and is a former Chairperson of the Society's Education Committee. Dr. Blakely is the author of several books, articles, and monographs on community development in the United States and in the Third World.

Hans B. C. Spiegel is a well-known urbanologist who has published numerous books and articles in the fields of public policy, planning, and sociology. He is a Professor of Urban Affairs at Hunter College in New York City.

Dean MacCannell is an Associate Professor of Community Development in the Department of Applied Behavioral

Sciences at the University of California, Davis. He is the Director of the Macro Structural Accounting Project. Dr. MacCannell has written three books in the fields of sociology and social theory. His most recent work, *The Tourist,* has received national recognition as an outstanding contribution to modern social thought.

Donald E. Voth is Associate Professor of Rural Sociology in the Department of Agricultural Economics and Rural Sociology at the University of Arkansas in Fayetteville. He is the author of a number of important papers in the area of evaluation and social action research. Dr. Voth has published in *Social Forces* and the *Journal of the Community Development Society.*

Edmond W. Alchin is a Community Development Specialist in the Cooperative Extension Service, Michigan State University.

Pairat Decharin is affiliated with Michigan State University. He is professionally employed as a Community Development Specialist in Thailand.

Howard Schutz is a Professor of Consumer Sciences at the University of California, Davis. Dr. Schutz specializes in community attitudes toward the quality of goods and services.

Jerry A. Moles is Assistant Professor of Anthropology at the University of California, Davis. Dr. Moles interest is in agricultural development and its impacts on local communities.

James G. Kelly was Dean of the School of Community Service and Public Affairs at the University of Oregon. Dr. Kelly is a board member of the Community Psychology Association and a frequent contributor to the *Journal of Community Psychology.*

PREFACE

This book is intended for community development specialists or students studying the community process who intend to enter the helping professions in some community-oriented context in such fields as community planning, social work and community health. Although the book is directed toward the so-called "development specialist," it is intended for a wide range of practitioners who intend to do research and/or promote action in community or group situations.

This book was written because of an apparent void in material useful to both teachers and practitioners on community development research concepts and strategies. The lack of a comprehensive reference source on this subject is somewhat perplexing, since all community-based work supposedly flows from some form of research or analysis of the community's ecology before programs are organized to meet community needs. Nonetheless, there is a dearth particularly of conceptual material to orient students or trainees in development to the variety of methods useful in community development research.

This book is not a "cookbook" for conducting research in community setting. Although such a book could be written, we feel that it would be of marginal utility and almost impossible to fit to the variety of needs and issues that arise in communities across the United States and around the world. Furthermore, we feel that an overview of community development research is needed and that subsequent volumes might articulate particular strategies more definitively. The book is, of course, not all-inclusive. Many excellent social science tools are not covered in this book.

Perhaps this volume will stimulate others to offer more work in the area of formulating and articulating research strategies in community development. We recognize that we are "sticking our necks out" by offering a book on community development research. Wise men and women counseled us against it. However, we felt that someone had to start somewhere.

This book is organized and written primarily as a teaching tool for upper division and graduate students and professionals. The expectation is that it will be used by teachers who are helping students to develop research skills. Therefore, it incorporates few illustrations of research *per se* and concentrates more on the research act or process and how the researcher uses his or her tools to make sense out of the reality that surrounds them.

Hopefully, readers will suggest ways to improve and expand this book in order to make it a more useful tool to future generations.

Edward J. Blakely

ACKNOWLEDGMENTS

This book would not have been possible if it had not been for the inspiration and guidance of the Education Committee of the Community Development Society of America. It is not an official publication of the Society, but it springs from that organization and its members. The principal contributors to this work are all members of the Society. Special thanks go to Earl Pettyjohn and Martin Pond, past Chairpersons of the Education Committee.

We are also indebted to the Department of Applied Behavioral Sciences at the University of California, Davis, for cooperation, assistance, and criticism in the preparation of the book. Finally, Dr. Orville Thompson, Chair of the Department of Applied Behavioral Sciences, deserves particular mention because of his consistent support of community development in general and community-oriented research in particular.

The Authors

INTRODUCTION

Although the contributors to this book worked independently, there is a unifying theme and thrust. As the reader will quickly identify, the book describes the research act and process in community development as part of the action. That is, research flows to and from action. It is not an isolated activity or insulated from the phenomena studied. The core of the research process in community development is moving concepts, that is people's visions or expectations to concrete and specific projects that will shape their lives in new and hopefully more rewarding directions.

Like almost all academic works, this book purposely remains on a theoretical plane. In our opinion, the theory, the framework, the concept and, ultimately, the values shape the process. Thus, we open the book with Hans Spiegel discussing this point. He offers a theoretical perspective on the community development act and a framework for understanding theory. He analyzes how theory or the lack of theory shapes the destiny of community programs and practitioners.

In Chapter 2 Dean MacCannell describes a theory-building method called macrostructural accounting. He summarizes this approach, its history, and its uses. He discusses how the theoretician, student, or practitioner can use this helpful research tool in developing perspective for himself or herself.

Dean MacCannell's and Hans Spiegel's work are a backdrop for Don Voth's chapter on action research. Don discusses the translation of theory into practice. He provides a transition, inasmuch as he builds a history and rationale for the action research strategy. In community development, the neat lines between experimental and control groups are difficult to draw. Thus the action research strategy provides a useful methodology for the community development scholar and/or practitioner.

The real question is, How do you do this type of research? In the next four chapters, Edward Alchin and Ed Blakely, with their coauthors, describe how one performs this type of research. Finally, Don Voth provides an interesting essay on the problem of evaluation research in community development. The authors all provide outlines, guides, and some examples. Obviously more illustrations would be helpful. The reader should review the bibliography and references in these chapters for more concrete illustrations.

The researcher is part of the process. Therefore, the final two chapters, by Jerry Moles and Jim Kelly, analyze the researcher's role. Jerry Moles examines the theoretical and philosophical position of the researcher attempting to merge ideals with application. Jim Kelly, on the other hand, pays particular attention to the power inherent in the position of information gatherer and organizer. All of us who read this work have asked ourselves, What are we researching? For whom? and, Why?

Chapter 1

TOWARD A SCIENCE OF COMMUNITY DEVELOPMENT

Edward J. Blakely

Community development is an emerging field of studies and practice. Although the field itself is young compared to other social science disciplines, it has its roots in fairly traditional social theory. To date, the codification of "a" development science with a community orientation has been relatively slow. Some observers suggest that the reason for this is a kind of antiintellectualism among community workers and a related hostility toward theory. Others suggest that community developers are too busy in the action to be concerned with "science-ing" the common sense of social intervention. Regardless of the view taken, there has been and continues to be a somewhat slow pace in the articulation of community development methods in academic or scholarly terms. This, of course, may be a blessing to the field; in its brief existence the number of theoretical debates and stratification of membership that occurs elsewhere in academic and proessional societies has not been great.

My own view is that while community development may not yet be a discipline, it is certainly a movement. It is difficult to generalize about the community development movement in quasiscientific terms, but some level of generalization is necessary to provide the reader with an overview or context for the statements made. There are some common traits in community development that serve as general underpinnings for the field; they might be stated as follows.

1. It is an applied behavioral science.
2. It is value centered and normative.
3. It is optimistic and humanistic.
4. It is oriented toward social/economic goals and uses anticipatory research strategies.
5. It is concerned with the total human climate or milieu.
6. It stresses the use of intervention through group and collective situations.
7. It is aimed at participation in its broadest sense.
8. It is concerned with the development of humanistic inter- and intrapersonal skills.
9. It views the community as a holistic and integrated network or system.
10. It is concerned with the ongoing management of change.

As an Applied Behavioral Science

The general intent of the applied social and behavioral sciences is to explore social systems in an effort to gain insights and understandings related to human behavior. Community development scientists use the community as a network of people, policies, programs, institutions, and cultures that are the focal point for inquiry and the base for the development of action or change strategems; the community is the laboratory for community development specialists. Consequently, the usual laboratory or controlled conditions that are applicable and useful for advancing theory in the traditional behavioral sciences are not appropriate or have only limited utility in community research.

Community research, as do other applied behavioral sciences, yields middle-range theories and hypotheses to validate initial assumptions or observations. The focus of research output in community development is designed to discover new applications of intervention strategies in governmental and social institutions that will improve the quality of community life. The definition of quality and community life derive largely from the setting itself (i.e., *barrio,* ghetto, neighborhood) and not from external sources or empirical evidence.

VALUE CENTERED AND NORMATIVE

Although much of modern science eschews the notion of values and assumes itself to be value free, community research is admittedly value laden. That is, community researchers acknowledge that the cultures of a community's social organizations or ethnic groups are part of the process of human social growth and must be addressed both in research and in action.

Community research, instead of being purely descriptive of the how and why of human behavior, is aimed at change in a predetermined value set direction. Change in community development terms is usually concerned with the client community's articulation of the direction or process that will substantially improve the quality and quantity of goods and services tc the community and improve human interaction and decision-making processes within the community. The normative nature of community research is demonstrated by theoretical and practical methods of diagnosing communities' needs, solving group and individual problems, organizing for action, and many prescriptive strategies to bring about or manage change.

OPTIMISTIC AND HUMANISTIC

Contemporary natural sciences and, to some extent, behavioral sciences have taken on a deterministic or almost fatalistic view as to the fate of humanity. Community developers are among those applied behavioral scientists who perceive that the potential for the future of humanity is not diminished because of current dilemmas. In fact, the community as a human institution (much like the family) represents a genuinely viable alternative for social interaction and problem solving.

Community developers accept the notion that people, regardless of race, sex, ethnicity, or place of birth, can find ways to solve their problems through group efforts. The community development movement is humanistic in orientation and subscribes to the belief that people's productive potential can be released through the design of more human institutions and organizations.

ANTICIPATORY AND ORIENTED TOWARD SOCIOECONOMIC GOALS

Social problems are manifest in modern society through enormous disparities in wealth and/or power. These differences act as a barrier to men and women all over the world in realizing their natural human potential. Community development is oriented toward the design of socioeconomic institutions that will close the gaps between human aspirations and currently available resources. Even though community developers use the tools of economists and are concerned with economic disparity, community development is not a predictive or deterministic science. Instead, community developers use research to explore the potential range of consequences of certain actions or the need for intervention, but the decision rests with the people in the community.

TOTAL CLIMATE OR MILIEU

Community developers intend in their interventions to alter the total environment and not just the physical setting and to change the residents' or clients' satisfaction by making isolated administrative rearrangements.

The total community conditions are taken into consideration in both the assessment of the need for change and the introduction of the strategy to bring it about. The atmosphere in which change is made is as important as the change itself. Therefore, the community must reach its goal, and it must be totally involved in all of the frustrations as well as successes in arriving at the objective. It is in this process that growth in "community" (relationships among people) occurs, and it is this process and not its outcome that stimulates and advances the science of community development.

GROUPS AS THE BASE FOR CHANGE

Since community development is oriented toward the community as a social entity, it follows that groups as represented by interest, race, class, sex, or concerns would be the focal point for study and action. In fact, community development has contributed substantially, directly and indirectly, to the other applied behavioral sciences in the understanding of group action.

The concerted effort of people in collective settings is the principal strategy in all community development efforts. Therefore, community developers study group behavior in community settings in an attempt to identify new avenues for catalyzing citizen awareness and community action.

PARTICIPATION

The use of groups and group strategies implies participation. Participation for the sake of participation is not the goal of community development. There is no magic about people entering into group situations. In fact, the evidence is that random or poorly organized participative efforts may be worse that no participation. Thus, community development scholars and practitioners attempt to improve the vehicles for participation and add methodologies to the participating process that enhance citizen input and decision making. Community developers have pioneered in the area of broad-scale group processes that provide a means for citizens to be heard directly in town meetings or indirectly through community surveys and the like.

INTER- AND INTRAPERSONAL COMPETENCIES

Participation and group processes cannot take place unless people are skilled in the methods of making groups work effectively. In this framework, community developers attempt to develop for themselves and for others the capacity to understand and react meaningfully to other people. The community developer must possess the power of observation necessary to perceive himself or herself in relation to others and to understand and evaluate his or her reactions (inwardly and outwardly) to others in relationship to his or her central reference point of the self.

Intrapersonal competencies are the skills required to deal with others in face-to-face relationships. This implies a genuineness or authenticity in relationships that permits open, honest communication and feedback.

Interpersonal relations in this context refers to the skills required to work in a vast framework of people with different, frequently opposing views and to understand them on their terms. This ability allows the development specialist to perceive and cope with conflict as a natural phenomenon in group settings.

Conflict is not seen as destructive or divisive, but as a necessary (if painful) part of the growth process. Development specialists attempt within the conflict situation to place the stress on problem solving as opposed to win-lose strategies and attitudes. The community developer's role is to provide avenues for the problem to be confronted objectively and dealt with intelligently. Personality and personal differences, while not overlooked or submerged, are not the focus of the specialist; the problem and the group's ability to see and resolve it are his or her goals.

SYSTEMS APPROACH

The community is a social system with many of the characteristics of any other living system. It has needs, beliefs, resources, and frailties similar to those of individual people. The components of the community system may not be as well defined as the human organism it represents but, in abstract form, the analogy holds. Therefore, the community developer approaches his or her work with the assumption that any movement or alteration in one part of the system has ramifications for other components. Research in community settings must therefore proceed from a "holistic" framework and not from the more segmented approaches of related social sciences.

Systems concepts and methods pervade all aspects of community development work. As a consequence, the design of projects or programs in community development requires considerable preplanning or diagnostic work to insure that the total system is being considered adequately and that change will bring about the desired and a desirable result.

MANAGING CHANGE

Community developers are sometimes accused of "social engineering." This accusation and similar accusations that development specialists are manipulators have little substance. Change in a community will take place regardless of the presence of development specialists. The question is, Are the changes taking place being managed by the community, or is the community managed by the change? The development specialist's role is to provide education, information, and resources so that local people can perceive their own needs and manage their destiny in a manner beneficial to themselves. How this is achieved is the focus of the development specialist's expertise as an observer and recorder. All communities need to know whether any action achieved the intended objective. Therefore, records are important; the knowledge of where a group started, the stages it progressed through, and the like may be of benefit to that community or to other communities.

SUMMARY

Community development is an applied behavioral science. It is grounded in the contemporary behavioral/social science theory of humanity. The principal concern of community development science is to understand how social theory can be effectively translated into social action. In the following chapters, the research paradigms for the concepts articulated here are explored. The reader may want to cross reference regularly the ideas stated here with the research strategies suggested in the balance of the book.

Chapter 2

THEORETICAL RESEARCH AND COMMUNITY DEVELOPMENT PRACTICE

Hans B. C. Spiegel

Community development has no shortage of theory. Every time someone indulges in a conventional wisdom about community development, such as "citizens will generally implement community decisions that they, themselves, helped to formulate," he or she is hip deep in community development theory. An assumption is made about community development knowledge and practices, and a generalization is built on that assumption. And that, to my way of thinking is using—or misusing—theory. The theory may or may not stand the tests of scholarly examination, of predictability, and of time. It can be found to be incorrect, as was the theory that, because everybody saw a concurving surface, the world is flat like a pancake. It took Galileo to challenge that theory. If theoretical researchers need a patron saint, they could do much worse than elevating Galileo, because he successfully stripped away the existing body of knowledge and discovered a new basic pattern that stood the test of scientific observations.

Regardless of the subject to be examined, theoretical research is a treacherous business. The core of theoretical research is composed of intellectual muckraking that involves manipulating abstracted evidence, generalizing experience, or discovering underlying principles—an enterprise ripe for sharp disagreements. When the topic under consideration is the community and its development, theoretical research becomes particularly difficult. Since everybody lives in communities, everybody has considerable community experience. Like the proverbial fish swimming in water and pragmatically "understanding" the water, so the general public and especially professionals with a community focus (e.g., politicians, human services personnel, and clergy) "know" the community. They know how to use the community for their own ends; they have successfully tapped one aspect of community theory, and most of the time it delivers in pragmatic terms. There is no shortage of conventional wisdom about communities and how they grow and change.

In this chapter, therefore, I address myself to community development practitioners who are interested in improving the craft by utilizing theory and by engaging in their own theory building. First, I discuss the idea of theory and how it is connected to descriptive data and to action. Then I show how public policy is formulated; I present both theories about program efficacy and assumptions about workable politics. Finally, I propose a simple method that might help practitioners to explore theoretical aspects of their own activities. In writing these pages I confess to a personal bias. I believe that "theory" must be demythologized and that "theorizing" must become an activity in which practitioners can and should participate actively. "Community development theory" is not the exclusive property of academicians, just as "community development practice" cannot be considered only by workers in the field. Much of the development of community development will depend on the systematic integration of experience and theory.

THEORY AND DESCRIPTION

A careful description about a community institution or event can be very useful for the community development practitioner. A description answers the questions of what happened, who was involved, what did they say, when did it occur, and so on. But even after much descriptive data have been compiled (and intriguing correlations established), descriptive research by itself cannot interpret the information and suggest why events happened the way they did and what is likely to happen in the future. To understand what is going on in the community, the descriptive data must be put into a framework that will help to order and explain them. Theory is the intellectual container that helps to interpret empirical data and generalize on them.

An example of descriptive reporting is the recent book by Studs Terkel, *Working: People Talk About What They Do All Day and How They Feel About What They Do* (1974). Terkel interviewed several dozen people working at various enterprises and wrote down what they said about their jobs. It is a fascinating document of individual perceptions of work. Terkel is careful to let each worker speak for himself or herself. He deliberately does not interpret, analyze, or editorialize. He describes. And the description helps the reader to appreciate the variety of jobs that Americans do and how they feel about it—now. It is like taking a few frames out of a movie drama and enlarging them as still photographs that show remarkable detail.

At about the same time, Stanley Aronowitz wrote *False Promises: The Shaping of American Working Class Consciousness* (1973). The topic is similar to Terkel's. But Aronowitz wastes little time with description of the here-and-now and moves quickly into a wide-ranging analysis of the history of labor, the youth culture, the psychology of play, and the like, and presents a theoretical framework that accommodates these various facets. Aronowitz provides a theoretical container that explains why things happened the way they did.

Both books should be read by the student of the working class. Although they supplement one another, they are different books with different purposes. Terkel gives voice to workers' own descriptions of their task; Aronowitz interprets and tries to account for observed behavior.

Robert Merton has given a telling example that differentiates empirical research from theory. He cites the "statistical uniformity" that, generally, Catholics seem to have a lower suicide rate than Protestants (Merton, 1968, p. 150). By itself, this observation is not a theory. All manner of data can be analyzed, aggregated, quantified, and correlated without producing theory. The question of causal "why's" must first be asked. Merton would qualify as theory building the above observation about Catholic-Protestant suicide differentials if it included the following "why-type" propositions derived from Durkheim.

1. Social choesion provides psychic support to group members subjected to acute stresses and anxieties.
2. Suicide rates are functions of unrelieved anxieties and stresses to which persons are subjected.
3. Catholics have greater social cohesion than Protestants.
4. Therefore, lower suicide rates should be anticipated among Catholics than among Protestants. (Merton, 1968, p. 151)

Although careful observation, description, and analysis are, of course, basic to the advancement of knowledge, theory does not automatically spring from these activities.

A mountain-top view of related evidence and related theories are required to formulate generalizable theory. Thus, theory becomes the conceptual capstone that integrates and accounts for the bodies of knowledge on which it is based.

The process of arriving at community development theory is both analytical and synthetic. Theory building is an intellectual striptease in which the body of knowledge and practices in community development are openly and unmercifully scrutinized and analyzed to see what is underneath all the outer trappings. It is also a synthesizing and generalizing experience that affords a broad view of many related bodies of knowledge. Theory has to explain both the makeup of a single community development episode as well as the entire social fabric in which community development is embedded; the view is near (as through a microscope), and far (scanning the surrounding conceptual territory).

TOWARD A DEFINITION OF COMMUNITY DEVELOPMENT THEORETICAL RESEARCH

A number of terms have been used above to describe a general stance toward community development theoretical research: a microscopic view (analytical), a mountain-top view or overview (synthetic), underlying principles, accounting for phenomena, basic patterns, abstracting and generalizing evidence, intellectual container, and so forth. This can be put less dramatically and more academically in the following attempt at a comprehensive definition.

Theoretical research in the context of community development is represented by the systematic inquiry that analyzes and synthesizes available data about the community and accounts for them in abstract and generalizable concepts that focus on the interplay between (1) patterns of community structure and behavior, and (2) the deliberate and organized interventions to help catalyze, guide, or develop these patterns.

There are a few elements in this definition that should be underlined. For one thing, research is not a casual activity of data gathering, but a systematic and often painful inquiry. This truism is readily accepted for descriptive or evaluative research, but some people feel that the theoretical researcher searches for only inductive insights. Second, as already pointed out, theoretical research deals with both analytical and synthetic processes. Third, the lodestone of theoretical research is that it accounts for phenomena, giving them an explanation and a rationale. As we will discuss, theory tries to answer the question Why does it occur this way? instead of What's happening? Fourth, theoretical research deals with a fairly high level of abstraction and generalization. In a sense, of course, everything spoken or written is an abstraction because the word is not the thing, but theory climbs to some of the top rungs on the abstraction ladder to deal with well-messaged intellectual concepts.

Finally, the definition puts the theoretical research into a community development framework. Since my view of community development presumes an interactive process between a community system and a deliberate intervener, I have postulated the definition accordingly. Theoretical research in community development focuses on the interplay between community and intervener, and not on the community by itself or on the study of the intervening actor without the community context. The community development researcher *must* know about the community and the intervening actor individually, but a community *development* scholar must penetrate the process that brings them together.

A scholar who exemplifies this stance is Roland Warren. In his many writings (see Warren 1970, 1972) he deals with the major issues of community development, such as community power, decision making, change strategies, community interorganizational dilemmas, and community planning. He moves beyond the question of describing what is, was, or could have been to the more difficult issues of *why* the community functions the way it does in relation to the various forces that try to shape and mold it.

THE THEORY-ACTION LINK

Even in community development circles one still hears about something working in theory, but not in practice. That is, of course, a classical *non sequitur*. If something works in theory, but not in practice, either the theory or the practice are wrong. Many people still believe that there is considerable dissonance between the world of theory and the world of concrete practice, with theory taking flighty trips into the irreality of the abstract and practice, including community development practice, responding to the cold here and now. In only one case am I willing to concede that the abstract and the concrete can be disassociated. It deals with the community development worker who was eager to demonstrate the advantages of cement sidewalks in the rural community to which he was assigned. He was on his knees, putting the finishing touches on the still wet section of sidewalk by smoothing out the settling cement, when half a dozen children ran barefooted across his newly fashioned sidewalk. "I like children," he grumbled to himself, "in the abstract, but not in the concrete."

In community development, action and theory should be closely entwined. One feeds on the other. As Kurt Lewin used to say, there is nothing so practical as a good theory. The practitioner should welcome theoretical knowledge and be capable of utilizing it to improve his or her performance in the field. On the other hand, the theoretician should eagerly check his or her formulations with the practitioner and construct and reconstruct theories in the light of empirical observations. This is easily said, but the fact remains that the action-theory link that should be inextricable is often badly frazzled and sometimes completely severed. Why should this be so?

There are, of course, many reasons. I will dwell on only two: (1) much action (and social policy) proceeds on the basis of presumed theory in the guise of unexamined conventional wisdom, and (2) much action is casually pulled together into presumed theory that turns out to be self-serving.

A number of community development activities proceed on the basis of assumptions and theories that must be questioned. Elsewhere, I listed five generally accepted community development assumptions that may have outlived their usefulness (Spiegel, 1970). One of these assumptions is that "the community" is a unitary and identifiable unit that acts essentially as a single organism. From this commonsensical but threadbare assumption grow attempts by community development workers to deal with the community on a macrobasis, which tends to overlook the specialized needs of subcommunities.

As another example, take the theory that was current 50 years ago that discriminatory practices in the community can only yield to educational and therapeutic efforts because human behavior in a free society supposedly is more governed by folkways than stateways. A third example of the oversimplistic theory is that a developing country's economy would benefit if its products were not exported to industrialized nations and were consumed instead in the domestic market. Thus, a community development specialist might advise Brazil to stop exporting coffee to Europe and the United States and utilize the former coffee-producing lands to raise protein-rich foods for Brazilians. However, as a result of such policies, the Brazilian economy would soon suffer and the action based on a humanitarian rationale would prove to be counterproductive (Boserup, 1975, p. 2).

Community development workers and social planners are quick to invent theories that "fit" their unique experiences. A generation ago, many community reformers believed that "slums inevitably cause crime, delinquency, disease, and other morbidities" (Abrams, 1966, p. 28) and that if the slums could be replaced by decent, safe, and sanitary housing, the human and housing problems of the poor would be basically relieved.

The planners of the War on Poverty were optimistic in 1964 that a combination of incremental redistribution of income, massive individual services to the poor, job training and job locating, and increasing the decision making by the poor about their own destinies could eradicate a major portion of American poverty. There was only limited evidence available about the usefulness of this mix of factors, but we used whatever data we could muster to conjure up theories—not often articulated as such—about the nature of poverty and the efficacy of eliminating it through a comprehensive program. As is well known today, too much was presumed (Ginzberg & Solow, 1974; Piven & Cloward, 1971, pp. 248–284). The War on Poverty did have its significant victories, but the enemy is far from defeated because of the lack of resources with which to fight and the relative lack of strategies, procedures, and programs based on valid theory. The War on Poverty was seriously hampered by the lack of theories.

In both the above categories, one becomes aware of the self-serving tendency to "fit" theory into the action mold that one is presently engaged in. There is a tendency for "pop theory" to replace the painstaking theoretical inquiry. Community development action and the public policy that supposedly guides such action is seldom triggered by scholarly theoretical formulations. Many factors, which may be political, economic, or historical-cultural, impact policy decisions; community development theory tags along as a not very potent partner. In part, this inability of community development theory to assert itself vis-á-vis the world of action is the fault of this theory's infancy. Relatively little is known that can be offered to the policymaker with assurance. And what little can be offered is veiled behind concepts that are difficult for the policymaker to penetrate; much is unfortunately lost in translating theory-oriented into action-oriented languages, even though these two worlds are interdependent.

THEORY AND PUBLIC POLICY

The creation of public policy affords important glimpses of the use, misuse, and nonuse of theory. As discussed community development theory probably does not play a major and articulate role in the formulation of community development programs. But theoretical considerations in subtle and intricate patterns weave in and out of the formulation of public policy and the planning of public programs. It may be instructive, therefore, to cite the example of the creation of the Model Cities Program in the Johnson Administration. (I was part of the planning of this program, first as a staff member of the White House task force that conceived the idea in 1965, and then as a member of the team that drafted the regulations in 1966.)

The Model Cities Program, like all public policy and programs, is inextricably embedded in a context. Its origins did not spring full-blown onto the scene. The context of the planning of the Model Cities Program included a historical moment in which reform was in the air: the poverty program had been launched, new educational legislation had just been passed, and new black militancy was manifesting itself; the government tried to respond to these pressures, and the "New Society" was on its way.

The President wanted to create a program that would reshape a number of American cities by way of a comprehensive program that would be equal to the "urban crisis" that was then being talked about. He created a Presidential task force to generate exciting new ideas and chose as members individuals from academia, Congress, and labor and industry who were not identified with traditional housing and urban development schemes of the past. Johnson instructed the task force not to be concerned about political and financial constraints, but to innovate.

What emerged from the task force was the outline of an ambitious program for a limited number of cities that would focus their efforts on specified poor neighborhoods and funnel considerable block grant funds into physical and social renewal endeavors, presided over by the local governing body, and carried out with the active participation of area residents. The proposed program was so comprehensive, expensive, and ambitious that when President Johnson finally released it "seasoned Congressional observers . . . smiled, shook their heads, and concluded that the master legislative strategist of the 20th century had bought a dud" and that, in the words of an Administration official, "we had lost our minds" (*New York Times,* November 4, 1966, p. 44).

Every meeting of the task force and almost every paragraph of its reports contained theoretical assumptions. Here are some of the questions that were thoroughly and sometimes heatedly discussed.

Should the program be administered by a quasipublic corporation, such as the Tennessee Valley Administration or Comsat, or through the existing governing structure of the city? (It was decided to channel the program through the governing body.)

Should the target areas receive a thorough physical treatment, relying principally on clearance of slum dwellings, or should rehabilitation of existing structures be stressed? (The second course was chosen.)

Should the hundreds of local antipoverty agencies be incorporated as resident representatives in the Model Cities Program, or should localities be able to choose their own organizations to assure "widespread citizen participation?" (Again, the second alternative won out.)

Is it more important to upgrade dramatically "the quality of urban life" through physical and social programs in the central city even at the risk of maintaining patterns of racial concentration, or is it more important to advance racial integration by making metropolitan housing choices and relocation assistance aggressively available? (Although considerable equivocating occurred on this issue, the former concern prevailed, after some modifications.)

And where were the considerations of theory in these deliberations? Articulated and explicit theory, as such, was not very much in evidence. For one thing, "urban theory" was and still is in a groping, preadolescent stage. There hardly was, or is, a body of "proven, scientific laws" to undergird urban affairs. No Newton or Einstein helped to guide the federal urbanists as the physical scientists were guided in the Manhattan Project in World War II. The questions posed by the task force did elicit more than merely individual biases and opinions. Some empirical data were available as gathered in mayor's offices and in universities about each of the above four issues, and this information was known to members of the task force and the staff. But these data were not firmly established and, in the end, could not be relied on to provide substantial guidelines for such a comprehensive task.

There certainly was no deliberate avoidance of theory in the task force; decisions were largely made on other than theoretical or "scientific" grounds. But, indirectly, theoretical considerations had impacted the lives of most members. The academic members, in particular, repeatedly articulated some of the fundamental policy dilemmas involved in the proposed program without being able to resolve them on theoretical grounds.

The program was finally distilled into the President's message to Congress where it was debated and, after the usual legislative compromise was passed into law. The process that occurred after the task force had made its report until enactment of the law was, of course, a political process. I use the term without derision; indeed, the political process illustrated the acting out of a number of ideological and fundamental concerns. Among the actors in this political drama were the White House, the mayors and other city officials throughout the country, the building and real estate interests, organized labor, racial and religious groups, antipoverty professionals, members of Congress, and even the drafters of the legislative package from the fledgling Department of Housing and Urban Development. These actors represented constituencies with interests that tugged and pulled at the policy to be formulated. Needless to say, peoples and institutions are quick to latch on to empirical and theoretical data that support their interests. However, to view the process of public policy formulation as merely engaging in empty and self-serving gesturing is an oversimplification. These actors bring a series of convictions and assumptions into a sometimes shrill public debate. When these assumptions are analyzed, they often contain internal consistency, a consistency that is perhaps surprising to the cynical observer who equates politics with pragmatic expediency.

THE ART OF MAKING FRIENDS WITH THEORY

The practitioner is often dismayed by the very mention of theory. Far from thinking that he or she can understand theory, practitioners may be dumbfounded when they are asked to link their actions to relevant theory. But both understanding and producing theory are possible—even necessary—for the community development worker. Here is one way in which practitioners and theory can become friends.

One way to think about engaging in theoretical research is to lean an abstraction ladder against the mountain of collected information and determine the type and level of basic ideas that emerge (Figure 2–1). Each rung of this ladder leads to more theoretical considerations. The ladder does not have to be climbed to the pinnacle to enjoy some of the benefits of abstractions; even a moderate climb of three or four rungs has its rewards.

The process of engaging in theoretical research, I said earlier, is both analytical and synthetic. The community development worker might, therefore, start with some analytical rungs at the bottom of the ladder and proceed to greater synthesis as he or she reaches further up. Even though the ladder in Figure 2–1 tends to start with the most immediate and action-oriented issues and moves upward toward the most abstract, the rungs are not always necessarily in sequence.

The first rung on this abstraction ladder is climbed after answering the question, What am I doing? As the practitioner describes his or her community development actions, a certain self-consciousness is almost bound to enter the mind. The very act of articulating one's actions is to engage in using verbal abstractions and symbols.

A second rung continues the self-conscious questioning about the practitioner's own actions. What other immediate actions preceded what I did? Immediately followed it? For example, the newly arrived community organizer on a city block asks a series of calculated questions of the candy store owner that in turn, are preceded by the observation that this particular store has considerable youth traffic.

A third rung might be represented by the collective

Figure 2-1 An abstraction ladder for practitioners.

Characteristic of each rung		Question to be asked
Formulation of theory	11	Can I make a generalization that suits me and that explains why the present and past actions happened the way they did to me and others?
Testing against existing theory	10	Can I explain what is happening on the basis of any existing theory?
Generating generalizable causal relationships	9	In general, how is the present action connected to one or more related happenings? Do the respective assumptions link together?
Articulation of basic assumptions	8	What assumptions is the present action, and comparable past actions, based on? What is behind professionals usually acting this way?
Comparability of observations	7	
Motivational, contextual analysis, beginning of force field analysis	6	Has that which is presently happening ever happened to me before? To others? In history?
Contextual description; Gestalt formation	5	Why do the various parties participate? Who gains what?
Motivational analysis of self	4	Who or what else is involved?
Classification, clustering	3	Why am I doing this?
Sequencing	2	Can I give a name to these various activities? Is there a common thread running through them?
Description of action; self-conscious personal examination of here-and-now	1	Is my action related to other things? What am I doing?

name that one gives to the sequence of activities one has undertaken. In the above example, perhaps one's initial observations and discussions in the candy store might be described as "reconnaisance," "getting the dope about the turf," or "starting to make contacts." This is a significant step, because one leaves here-and-now descriptions of isolated activities and clusters them under a given rubric. Classification has commenced.

Another rung might be scaled as one questions, Why am I doing this? What is the motivation behind my action? Are candy store-based informal data valuable? Do I ask these questions because of a personal idiosyncracy of being an outgoing, friendly person?

A fifth rung comes with a deliberate attempt to flesh out a broader context for my actions. Who else is involved? Can I draw up a cast of characters? Here we try to describe a social field in which the action takes place. In our example, it might be interesting to observe who the store owner appears to be, who else is in the store, the demographic characteristics of people coming in and out, and the relationship of the store to the sidewalk and the neighborhood beyond.

The fifth and sixth rungs try to analyze who the various actors are and why they behave as they do in this context. What motivates whom? Who gains what? Is the candy store owner's behavior primarily determined by a desire to make fat profits? To stay on the good side of the local youth? How do the various persons and institutions relate to one another? What is some of the social chemistry of this situation?

Rung seven seeks to compare the present observations with other personal experiences, professional experiences, and even with historical evidence. Community development in a democracy has antecedents that can teach important lessons. For example, small commercial interests, such as our candy store owner, have sparked many community actions, from Paul Revere's ride to immigrant self-help efforts in the 1800s. This rung attempts to broaden the contextual base horizontally and relate the here-and-now observation to similar events that happened at other times and other places.

The eighth rung seeks to articulate the assumptions that are held by various parties. What is the conventional wisdom on which actions are based? In our example, why is a visit to a popular communal spot, such as a neighborhood store, so important for the newly arrived community development worker? Is it that "average" citizens gather there, thus permitting beginning "soundings" of community sentiments? (The assumption may be misleading or outright mistaken, but if it is an important factor in the community development worker's behavior, it should be so articulated.)

As we climb our ladder toward the still more abstract, we come to rung nine, which questions whether any causal relationship usually exists between sequential activities. For example, is the stranger who enters the candy store usually cause for suspicious treatment by the proprietor and gathered customers? Or, to take a different community event, will the show of police force under certain specific circumstances usually result in overt and violent counteraction? This rung is a particularly perplexing one on which to stand, because one usually is not certain how securely it is fastened to the rest of the ladder. Causal relationships are not simple one-to-one equations, but multifaceted syndromes of factors. Still, the person interested in theory must risk the temptation of oversimplification and engage in the speculation of which actions cause which reactions.

The tenth rung will send the practitioner to the library, to the academicians, and to his or her colleagues. What existing theory is relevant to the things that are presently happening? This question presumes that someone, somewhere, knows enough about relevant theory to be responsive to the practitioner. It may take long, intensive conversations to search out theories, lodged as they frequently are in many related academic disciplines that may have relevancy. One of the few masterful efforts at translating existing theory to make it relevant to a community development program at the local level was performed by Marshall Clinard in *Slums and Community Development* (1966). Clinard was able to relate some of the more important theoretical and empirical studies of slum life and slum development to Delhi's urban community development program, pointing out implications for both theory and Delhi.

Finally, rung eleven asks the practitioner to formulate his or her own theory. It can be a theory that is taken from someone else and incorporated as one's own, or it may be a tailor-made theory that relies primarily on the practitioner's independent checking and rechecking of personally developed concepts and data. In either case, intellectual rigor must be present; a snap assumption will not suffice. It probably should go without saying that the theory, be it adapted or independently formulated, should be committed to paper. Even if it is not immediatley shared with others, the theory can thus be checked with the passage of time and altered accordingly.

Once the top rung has been scaled, the process of theoretical research has not ended. True, the practitioner who thus has gone through deliberate analysis and synthesis of his or her experiences is rewarded by the mountaintop panorama but, like Sisyphus, cannot tarry long before repeating the endeavor. Theory building is a continuous process. Once a theory "fits" a certain set of circumstances, it has to be tested against new situations and newly generated theories. These new data are then recycled through the procedure. It is important for the practitioner to remember that an integral part of this process is the relationship between the top rungs and the bottom rungs. Both are subject to change. If theory building does not help the practitioner to change his or her professional behavior (What am I doing?), the exercise is empty.

The above rungs of the abstraction ladder are not very different from the steps in any attempt at theoretical research. They are reproduced here in a simplified version because of the belief that theory must be demythologized to make it more attractive and useful to the practitioner. The above procedure may look like a mail-order do-it-yourself kit, but I would rather err on the side of stimulating "soft" systematic thought about theory than having the practitioner continue to hold theory in unexamined awe. As the title of this chapter implies, community development workers should and can learn to become friends with theory.

ANYONE CAN PLAY

There is much theory building to be accomplished in community development. The practitioner, as we have pointed out above, can perform crucial services to himself or herself and to the field as a whole by engaging in theory building. So can the professor of community development. Both practitioner and scholar can play at this game. The issues to be treated theoretically can have as their starting point a specific community development action or an esoteric concept about the nature of community intervention. Both issues can be subjected to theoretical research.

One is tempted to append here a whole host of community development issues that should be scrutinized with increasing theoretical rigor. Enough empirical data are presently available concerning some crucial community phenomena to move several rungs up our abstraction ladder. It should be possible, for example, to develop hypotheses and theories about decentralized delivery of governmental services (Hallman, 1974; Spiegel, 1974; Yin

& Yates, 1974); or about the variety of "life styles in the mosaic culture," to use Berry's phrase (1973), and their consequence for community development and planning; or about the implications of urban and rural governmental programs, such as the War on Poverty and Model Cities, on the participatory behavior of target area residents (Kramer, 1969; Rose, 1972; Warren et al., 1974).

One of the most perplexing community development problems has been "why some programs succeed by the developers' standards and other programs fail." (Saunders, 1970, p. 29) This inquiry is particularly significant for some large-scale comprehensive development efforts that require massive private and governmental funds. It is obvious that the public interest is not served if such large funds are spent on the basis of mere hunches or politicized judgments. One should be able to use existing experiences and build on them some generalizations that could help to guide the development process. The Ford Foundation (1973) ventured into this difficult arena and has begun to take a few telling steps up on the abstraction ladder. The Ford study examines the recent history of community development corporations. Here are some tentative conclusions.

> While there is no coherent theory of development or redevelopment for depressed rural and urban areas in an advanced economy, the national experience over the last decade and our own work over the last few years suggest two primary institutional characteristics:
>
> First, a greater impact on problems of distressed areas is likely to be made by a locally based, multipurpose institution—a community development corporation—than would result from government acting directly.
>
> Second, the early growth of such CDCs should be supported by a "development supported institution" able to provide grants for administration and project activities, equity and debt capital on subsidy terms, particularly for projects of scale and technical managerial assistance. (p. 8)

These two conclusions may seem overly modest and not very world shaking. True, no comprehensive theory about fighting poverty in America is involved here. But most theorizing, like everything else, moves by relatively small and incremental steps. In the above instance, a limited program was analyzed and two generalizations were made about how it might be improved. This theorizing may or may not meet the test of further inquiry or of future experiences. But, for the moment, this formulation by the Ford Foundation gives people who are interested in community development corporations something concrete to think about and to base their actions on.

Not only the Ford Foundation can engage in the process of theoretical research. Academic degrees and coffers full of money are not required to start climbing the abstraction ladder. Community development practitioners—even when they are slogging through the muddy arena of community controversy—can be helped by existing theory and, more important, can learn to theorize about their own immediate experiences.

BIBLIOGRAPHY AND REFERENCES

Abrams, C. *The city is the frontier.* New York: Harper & Row, 1966.

Aronowitz, S. *False promises: The shaping of American working class consciousness.* New York: McGraw-Hill, 1973.

Berry, B. J. L. *The human consequences of urbanization.* New York: St. Martin's Press, 1973.

Boserup, M. Sharing is a myth. *United Nations Development Forum,* 1975, 3 (2).

Clinard, M. B. *Slums and community development.* New York: The Free Press, 1966.

Community development corporations: A strategy for depressed urban and Rural areas. New York, A Ford Foundation Policy Paper, 1973.

Ginzberg, E., Solow, R. M. (Eds.) *The great society: Lessons for the future.* New York: Basic Books, 1974.

Hallman, H. W. Neighborhood power: A ten year perspective. *Neighborhood Decentralization,* November–December 1974.

Kramer, R. M. *Participation of the poor.* Englewood Cliffs, N.J.: Prentice-Hall, 1969.

Merton, R. K. *Social theory and social structure.* New York: The Free Press, 1968.

Piven, F. F., & Cloward, R. A. *Regulating the poor.* New York: Vintage Books, 1971.

Rose, S. M. *The betrayal of the poor.* Cambridge: Schenkman Publishing Co., 1972.

Sanders, I. T. The concept of community development. In Lee J. Carey (Ed.), *Community development as a process.* Columbia, Mo.: University of Missouri Press, 1970.

Spiegel, H. B. C. Changing assumptions about community change. *Journal of the Community Development Society,* 1970, 2 (2).

Spiegel, H. B. C. (Ed) *Decentralization,* Volume 3 in Citizen Participation in Urban Development series, Fairfax, Va., NTL Learning Resources Corporation, 1974.

Terkel, S. *Working: People talk about what they do all day and how they feel about what they do.* New York: Pantheon Books, 1974.

Warren, R. L. *The community in America.* (2nd ed.) Chicago: Rand McNally, 1972.

Warren, R. L. The good community—What would it be? *Journal of the Community Development Society,* 1970, 1 (1).

Warren, R. L., Rose, S. M., Bergunder, A. F. *The structure of urban reform.* Lexington, Ky.: Lexington Books, 1974.

Yin, R. & Yates, D. Street-level governments: Assessing decentralization and urban services. *Nation's Cities,* November 1974.

THE ELEMENTARY STRUCTURES OF COMMUNITY: MACROSTRUCTURAL ACCOUNTING AS A METHODOLOGY FOR THEORY BUILDING AND POLICY FORMULATION*

Dean MacCannell

Important research on small communities was begun by a group at Cornell University in the early 1960s. (For a recent summary of this research, see Young & Young, 1973). Now known as "macrosocial accounting," this research is noteworthy for its sheer volume of 50 dissertations and monographs that have appeared in the past 15 years; over 100 research reports were published during the same period. A striking feature of all this work is its genuinely cumulative nature. The approach is based on a simple set of variables and hypotheses, and each succeeding study addresses a question raised in earlier research work. This research has been instrumental in the formation of a series

*Support in writing this chapter was provided by the Macrosocial Accounting Project of the Agricultural Experiment Station at the University of California, Davis.

of empirical discoveries of regularities in the structure and behavior of entire communities. The quality of the theory that is being developed through this research is on a par with other interesting and innovative theory in the social sciences and is specifically related to recent developments in central place theory, graph theory, semiotics, and structuralism. This chapter will provide an intelligent, layperson's introduction to the macrosocial accounting approach as one approach to community development theory building. In the previous chapter Hans Spiegel developed the steps for theory generation. In this chapter I will articulate the methods for that process.

There are three central themes in macrostructural work: differentiation, centrality, and solidarity.

DIFFERENTIATION

A principal idea formed in the early days of macrosocial accounting that proved significant beyond expectation was that basic elements of communities are not individuals but groups, facilities, neighborhoods, institutions, organizations, and community-level systems of transportation, education, refuse removal, markets, recreation, and the like. An early research thrust was designed to determine the relationship between these elements. This exploratory work examined within a single framework officially constituted organizations such as planning boards, voluntary organizations (consumer cooperatives), and grass-roots movements (Young & Larsen, 1965). The capacity of the paradigm to handle these diverse types of groups was probably the basis for the survival and growth of macrosocial accounting systems during the late 1960s when radical graduate students were abandoning established research approaches. During the early period, then, innovative strategies were developed to describe and measure the relationships between community elements *directly* using key informant surveys and available data that could be obtained from novel sources such as aerial photographs and telephone directories. This move sidestepped the use of expensive sample surveys that would have been time consuming and would also have provided only indirect access to community structure. Once analysis of component groups was begun, it became quite clear that communities are only expressions of underlying structural codes similar in some respects to the genetic code or to a grammar of a language.

In a series of several hundred small communities in Latin America and upstate New York, it was found that groups, institutions, services, and facilities of communities exist in relatively stable matrices. For example, a reexamination of the structure of the Yucatan communities studies by Robert Redfield (1950) and his associates revealed the simple pattern shown in Figure 3–1. It is evident that things such as schools, medical services, and recreational facilities do not appear at random but in association with other specific institutions and services.

This pattern of systematic elaboration of community institutions is called *social structural differentiation* of communities and has been accurately measured using Guttman scales of community attributes. Although the specific institutions that enter into the matrix vary from culture area to culture area, the general pattern of differentiation has been found in every study using macrosocial accounting techniques; the pattern has been replicated in studies in Taiwan, Ghana, India, the Philippines, Laos, North America, South America, and elsewhere.

When structural differentiation was first detected, it led to some initial concern that an established way of thinking about community development may not be correct. The current notion in and outside of social scientific circles is that development can be induced by the mere implanta-

Figure 3-1   Level of differentiation of communities studies by Robert Redfield. (Adapted from Young and Fujimoto, 1965. 1 indicates presence of the item, 0 indicates absence.)

| | Urban ⟵——————————————⟶ Folk | | | |
	Dzitas	Tepoztlan	Chan Kom	Tusik
Community is autonomous and has a name	1	1	1	1
There is an elementary school in community	1	1	1	0
Meat is butchered in the community	1	1	1	0
A priest resides in the community	0	1	0	0
There is a hotel or an inn in the community	1	1	0	0
There is a pool hall or other commercial recreation	1	1	0	0
A doctor is resident in the community	1	0	0	0
There is a theater where movies are regularly shown	1	0	0	0

1 = present   0 = absent

tion or buildup of a particular institutional sector such as the educational or the economic sector. For example, there is no reasonable way to explain the specific connection between medical doctors and pool halls in Latin American communities, yet there is a regularly occurring relationship between them. The relationship between education and economic growth is more acceptable from the standpoint of common sense but, in the light of these findings about differentiation, it became suspect; perhaps there is a low-level empirical association similar to the relationship between pool halls and medical doctors (Spencer, 1973). It seemed to make more sense to try to determine what other variable characteristics of entire communities are associated with alterations of the total pattern of social structural differentiation.

In addition to providing basic information on community structure, the discovery of differentiation was also seen as having potential for applied programs and policy formation. Before moving on to the subsequent study of other underlying characteristics of community structure, it is worthwhile to mention some early thoughts on applications that grew out of the research on differentiation. Referring once again to Figure 3–1, it can be seen that a recommendation to locate a medical doctor in Chon Kom is tantamount to a recommendation that a pool hall and a hotel be built and a priest brought there as well. Moreover, there may be certain other institutions, not analyzed but fitting the same pattern, that are also a part of the matrix surrounding the establishment of medical services. It was felt that applied social scientists might be able to make use of information about community differentiation to maximize the probable success of their programs. An effort to upgrade medical service delivery to Chon Kom, for example, might meet with more success if the recommendation was for something other than a resident doctor; perhaps a circuit-riding mobile clinic could provide necessary services without requiring elaboration of social structure on a local level.

Another thought on applications that grew out of research on social structural differentiation centered on deviations from the matrix. For example, Dzitas deviates from the expected pattern in that it does not have a resident priest. Such an anomaly might signal the existence of an alternative system of religious service delivery that has grown up naturally in the community and is functionally equivalent to the presence of a priest. If Chon Kom undergoes development, as Redfield claimed it planned to do, it might profitably examine the organization of religion in Dzitas as an alternative to the resident priest. (Of course, the absence of a service might indicate a real lack of it, in which case the "alternative model" is doing without). We have no idea whether any of these thoughts found their way into applications in the early 1960s, or even that they should have, given the crude state of the art at that time. However, it is important to record that a detailed concern for possible applications was explicit from the beginning.

As already indicated, the discovery of a stable pattern of differentiation of communities is interesting in its own right, and it appears to have potential for application, but it also raises some questions. Why are some communities more differentiated than others? What makes a community move up and down the differentiation ladder or stay in place?

CENTRALITY

It was assumed from the beginning of the development of macrosocial accounting systems that community structure and change are, in part, functions of a wider sociocultural context. Crops, for example, provide a year-round activity, providing hypothetically specific relations between land-owners and agricultural workers and between work and technology (Young, 1976). These general practices and relationships provide overall organization for all the communities in a particular agricultural area. Some systems of communities have been analyzed as such before the invention of macrosocial accounting (e.g., the Kula ring, marketing centers, and their satellite communities). This type of research suggested that, in addition to communities being passively united in a cultural matrix, they also actively relate to each other through ongoing transactions (trade, cooperation, population movements, warfare, etc). Modern examples of community systems are easy to provide: cooperating communities in regional planning groups, the towns in the Tennessee Valley Authority, and the stops in an interurban regional transit system. Some such systems are relatively stable, either in steady state or growing and declining slowly and evenly. Other systems, suburban Southern California, for example, are in a state of constant excitement and generate a steady stream of experimental social relations, alternative life-styles, and new kinds of human structures.

Of course, some communities in these systems develop beyond their regional identity and become cosmopolitan centers with connections in the world beyond their local area. And some communities do not fully represent local structure, being consigned, even within the region, to a limited role; migrant labor camps are an example. It is hypothesized that under conditions of system stability (see above), the level of differentiation of the component communities varies with their centrality in the wider system. In other words, the larger communities with more diversified institutions internally are the most central, with the most diversified contacts with the region and the wider world. Conversely, the communities with little or no institutional elaboration internally are remote and are tied to the wider world only through the central communities in their system. Figure 3–2 shows the hypothetical relations between community differentiation and centrality in a stable modern system.

The relationship in Figure 3–2 is not intended to be a precisely calibrated model. There are important deviations from this pattern. It is important to keep in mind, however, that the positive linear relationship between differentiation and centrality described in Figure 3–2 is a correct generalization. There is ample evidence that communities and community systems are ordinarily structured in this way and that it is possible to make generalizations about centrality in the context of increasing differentiation.

Figure 3-2 Relationship between community differentiation and centrality in a developed system (hypothesized).

	Differentiation	Centrality
Centrality stages (see text)	Three or more ethnic can influence the community as a whole (i.e., swing an election)	Community has its own television station where programming originates
Stage 3	Community has suburbs and/or detached bedroom subcommunities	Community has a fully developed middle class (i.e., the middle class has its own shopping areas, schools, neighborhoods)
	Three or more different types of industrial plants are in or near the community	Freeway or railway enters the community, or the community has its own airport
	Community has specialized services: bank, doctor, lawyer, college, etc.	Community contains branches of regional and national organizations (the Democratic Party, NOW, etc.)
Stage 2	Community has its own primary and secondary schools	There is a central gathering place (meeting hall, auditorium) in which general meetings on matters relating to entire community are held periodically
	One or more organization or group beyond the household, church, or union has formed	A segment of the local population knows the ways of the wider society (understands basic professional standards, business principles, secular ethics, etc.)
Stage 1	A viable settlement exists (i.e., a local group has formed around some activity)	Community has a name that is known both in community and in the wider region

At the lowest levels of differentiation, the community is a mere settlement that demands neither attention nor loyalty from its residents. This is the situation of certain mountain settlements, coves, hamlets, woodlots, bayous, Indian reservations, and Appalachian mountain groups. These are often single-family or dual-family groupings with ties based more on kinship than on any "sense of community." They are stagnant, isolated, and xenophobic, laden with irrational traditions and intense emotion.

A clearly defined second development stage is entered when a community establishes itself as an entity in the minds of its own people. This is the stage during which one hears a great many expressions of concern for the quality of the community's services, its "spirit," and/or its reputation. In the United States, communities at the second level of centrality are influential in the lives of their own citizens, but not in the wider world, and they are often thought of as "good little towns" or "good places to rear children." They are also sometimes seen as square, chauvinistic, smug, and oppressive.

A third stage of centrality is reached when the community extends its influence to the entire region of which it is a part. Market towns, county seats, places where courts, regional offices of the Department of Motor Vehicles, and the like, are located are examples. Places like Stockton, California and Grand Island, Nebraska are at this third level. Finally, some communities dominate their regions completely and extend their sphere of influence regionally, nationally, and globally. Zurich and Las Vegas are examples of relatively small cities that are important beyond their immediate community system.

At least one line of theory, originating with Durkheim, would suggest that we are not dealing with two distinct variables. According to this view, as a community increases its complexity, it *necessarily* increases its internal and external communication ties or it will fall apart. While macrosocial accounting recognizes covariation of differentiation and centrality as an empirical regularity, the existence of ghost towns suggests that the two are, in fact, separate dimensions of community structure that can vary independently. Figure 3–3 is a typology of community structures based on the independent variation of differentiation and centrality. (The "normal" cases are double-outlined.)

SOLIDARITY

A third dimension of structure that is important in community and regional change is social structural solidarity. Structural solidarity is not to be understood in the same terms as individual commitment or attachment to community. Often there are ironical twists in solidarity as we move from the individual to the community level. For example, the kinds of communities that have commanded the fiercest loyalties from their members, those found in primitive societies, are very fragile and sometimes fall apart as soon as

Figure 3-3   Typology of community structures based on the interaction of differentiation and centrality.

Centrality stages	Low	Differentiation Medium	High
I	Isolated settlements	Tourist resorts on faraway island	Remote Air Force bases and isolated scientific stations
II	"Intentional" communities	Small town ("good" little towns)	Oil and mining "boom" towns
III	Organized urban ethnic enclaves	Suburbia	Market centers and small cities

they are modernized. Interestingly, these same moderns, who collectively have the power and organization to break up and absorb every known type of community, are also the most alienated, disaffected, unloyal, unattached, and uncommitted people in history.

The empirical form of social structural solidarity is a group-level system of values, ethics, standards, and operational guidelines. Some of these systems, such as religions and political ideologies, achieve great generality and permit entire cultures to organize information, attitudes, and programs within a single integrative format. Examples of macrosolidarities include communism, Protestantism, capitalism, and scientific rationality. It is an interesting characteristic of these broad frameworks that they have the power to organize the behavior of even those individuals who do not "consciously believe" in them. For example, a good Catholic in a nation that values hard work and individual achievement can behave exactly as if he or she has the Protestant work ethic. Similarly, in our society, an anti-rational devotee of the occult will sometimes follow the scientific dicta of precision and accuracy in making astrological calculations. In other words, solidarity at the group level has a certain spirit or life of its own that is independent of any given individual expression of it. In addition to these macrosolidarities, there are the microsolidarities of family life and the mesosolidarities of community life.

Although similar groups may vary in terms of how solidary they are, there is no group that completely lacks solidarity. If a group, no matter how small, has no integrative format, program, or focus, it will dissolve into the surrounding social structure. This seems to have happened to many suburban communities, such as Orange County, California, that have lost their identity and have been subsumed into the surrounding urban matrix, not as a subcommunity to be dealt with as such, but as a vague memory in a sprawling structure.

In thinking about social structural solidarity of communities, it is helpful to imagine a solidarity *baseline* that is tied to community differentiation. This baseline of solidarity is the minimum necessary to keep a community *of a given complexity* together. It other words, it is necessary for communities and groups to run smoothly just to stay in place, and the more complex the structure, the greater the demands on the regulatory systems and systems of values that permit ongoing adjustments to a changing environment. Figure 3–4 presents a hypothetical illustration of the relationship of community differentiation to solidarity.

Figure 3-4   Illustration of the expected relationship between community differentiation and solidarity.

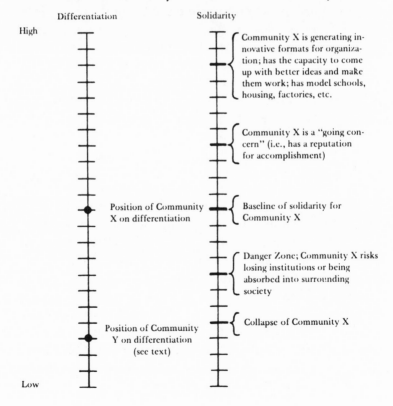

Note that the less differentiated community (Y) can be a going concern with a level of solidarity that would endanger the more differentiated community (X). This hypothesis contains an explanation for the mass movements of population into structurally simpler communities (X → Y) during times of crisis, as occurred recently in Bangladesh, during the European Middle Ages, and in the United States. Such movement seems to be an almost biologically motivated survival strategy for the species that permits us to live through times during which social problems increase at a rate faster than the development of adequate solutions.

It should go without saying that from the standpoint of macrosocial accounting theory, very complex social structures are by definition extended beyond existing integrative formats and are, therefore, always on the verge of dramatic collapse. The best illustrations of this are found in university life, especially in those colleges and departments that are thought to be "the best" in a certain field at a certain time. Juggling together recent intellectual trends, methodological advances, "star" professors, an accumulation of substantive findings that cannot be integrated into traditional frameworks, and complex research funding arrangements, and keeping all this together for any length of time, is an enormous task. Such moments of "collective effervescence" are of relatively short duration, usually lasting only until a second generation takes power, a second generation that was originally attracted to the place because it was great (i.e., trend followers, but not necessarily intellectual innovators).

So far I have written about solidarity as if it were the creation of its own group, a set of homegrown ideas that help to keep everyone and everything together. Some solidarity, such as that of the early Protestants, seems to work this way, but there is a second and more pervasive type of solidarity that should also be mentioned. Often, the wider society provides an integrative format for a subcommunity that it wants to assimilate on its own terms. The degraded identities of certain ethnic groups in American society are, in effect, ideological "gifts" from the dominant groups. I am speaking now of matters such as the perception of the black male as a "supermasculine menial" and other prevailing beliefs designed to "explain" and to "justify" the place of disadvantaged subgroups in American society. Elsewhere, I have termed this kind of passive solidarity, which results from filling a mold shaped by the dominant society, *negative solidarity* (MacCannell, in press). Here it is necessary only to note that negative solidarity is not limited to disadvantaged groups, but is spreading to all communities as they organize themselves according to state and federal guidelines.

The recent rise in black consciousness in the United States can be viewed, as it is within the movement, as positive solidarity; it is an effort to wrest the definition of Afro-American identity away from the image-making machinery of the dominating white majority. Or it can be viewed as negative solidarity, as a necessary reformulation of ethnic identity as black Americans depart the rural South for the urban North and West and begin to occupy a new structural niche. To be successful, a movement must be composed of both positive and negative forms of solidarity.

REINTERPRETING COMMUNITY CHANGE

What has been presented so far is a discussion of a minimal model of community structure necessary for the analysis and interpretation of social change at the community and regional levels. It is aesthetically pleasing to specialists because it covers salient aspects of community life and permits the formulation of testable hypotheses about change processes without requiring a series of tentative assumptions or resulting in a complex tangle of concepts. A more detailed second-stage model that incorporates additional variables (rigidity and involution) is currently undergoing testing and development by researchers using macrosocial accounting systems. A full discussion of this second stage is impossible here; this chapter is confined to interpretations of the change process possible within the original model.

Virtually any feature of community life that is thought to be important or meaningful by laypersons in their discussions of community change can be fitted into this simple model. In other words, aspects of community thought to be salient and somehow connected but only in a vague sense can now be fit together quite precisely. For example, the notions of community "spirit" or a "sense of community" are aspects of *solidarity*. A community's "isolation" or, alternatively, its "importance" are functions of its *centrality*. And *differentiation* incorporates what we ordinarily think of as level of economic or social development.

The model can lead beyond common sense to an expanded awareness of community structure and change. For example, a solidarity movement might be necessary for the survival of a given community. Viewed from the standpoint of the model presented here, a sudden shift of consciousness that causes everyone to become depressed about the community's situation and future might be viewed as a hopeful sign. It is often necessary for almost everyone to become convinced that a town is dying before enough concern can be mobilized to make it live. It has been empirically demonstrated, at least once, that communities with reputations for being "bad" towns behave and react much like communities with "good" reputations, and that these two types of town grow faster and adapt to change better than communities without specific reputations. To understand this it is again helpful to continue the interpretation in terms of social structural solidarity: a community has to have an extra measure of solidarity to have *any* reputation whatever, and it is this underlying solidarity that leads to superior adaptation, *independent* of the content of the image projected by the community (Young, 1964).

In a similar way, *centrality* provides an explanation of some radical changes that are currently occurring in central cities and their suburbs that have so far eluded common-sense explanation. Here we refer to the deterioration of the inner city and the simultaneous appearance in suburban communities of the emergence of small cities with industries, shopping centers, and social classes. From the standpoint of macrosocial accounting, the growth of urban communities is not a matter of simple expansion according to the Chicago School's concentric ring theory (Figure 3–5). The appearance of bedroom communities beyond the original suburban fringe creates the potential for a structural implosion. The addition of this outer ring displaces the center into the suburbs, draining institutions and people out of both rural areas and the original urban core. From the standpoint of any given suburban community that has recently undergone a sudden expansion, these changes, which affect every aspect of community life, cannot be traced to any preceding changes that occurred inside the community. The transformation is the result of the development of other communities and other communication ties that are often quite remote.

Differentiation provides a basis for assessing the likelihood that a particular service, institution, or group will locate in a given community. Since services, institutions, and groups are themselves aspects of community differentiation that line up in the unidimensional pattern shown in Figures 3–1 and 3–2, it is possible to predict accurately which of these a community will gain if it becomes more complex and which it will lose if it declines. The techniques for making these predictions have recently been worked out and are known within the macrosocial accounting

Figure 3-5   Comparison of expansion theory of urban growth and structural theory of shifting centrality.

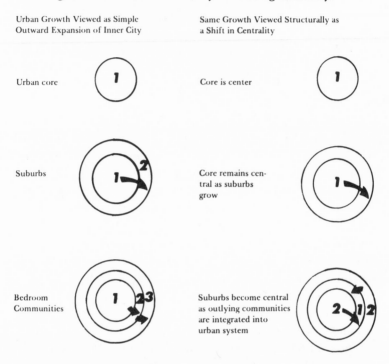

framework as procedures for "institution tracking" (Wheelock & Young, 1973).

These illustrations are intended to be merely suggestive, not exhaustive. Familiarity with macrosocial accounting provides a vocabulary and an approach to community structure and change and facilitates interpretation of many other kinds of community problems. Of course, close empirical analysis of community problems, program evaluation, and the development of plans for future structural change require the use of a functioning macrosocial accounting data bank. Such a bank would minimally contain measures of the three variables for the community in question and for the others in its regional system. Macrosocial accounting data banks are currently in operation for communities in New York State, southern Illinois, and Alabama, and are under development in California.

Troubleshooting a community system using a macrosocial accounting data bank is guided by the hypothesis that communities tend to occupy the same random differentiation, solidarity, and centrality relative to the other communities in the surrounding region. This would lead the analyst to examine the communities that are most out of alignment on one of the variables (communities high on solidarity but low on centrality, or low on differentiation, etc.) (See, for example, the communities that deviate from the normal pattern in Figure 3–3.) These are the stress points in the system, the places in which important changes or innovations are likely to originate; alternatively, these are the places most likely to produce a pathological adaptation, such as the string developments of used car dealers that attach overdeveloped suburbs to their system. The probable reaction of a community to misalignment in a system is usually evident once the behavior of the surrounding communities has been taken into consideration. The investigator should be able to make a reasonably accurate prediction as to whether the community will grow, decline, stay in place, shift its network position, or become more or less solidary.

Conclusion

It should be clear from the preceding remarks that macrosocial accounting provides a framework for understanding social change in communities and regions as a *naturally occurring process*. That is, it is assumed that social change occurs *independent* of the programs and policies of planners, administrators and, for that matter, of grass-roots organizers and revolutionaries. This is not the same as saying that organizers, administrators, revolutionaries, and the like make no difference in the change process. They do. However, from the standpoint of macrosocial accounting, they do not stand *outside* social structure where they exert independent, causal influence on the change process. They are fully caught up *in* the process. In short, it is possible to "track" revolutionaries or even mundane items such as comprehensive community plans, (i.e., to line up the structural characteristics of the communities in a system and pinpoint the areas that are ripe for revolution or ready for rational planning).

It is the hope of macrosocial accountants that a recognition of the inevitability of the recent appearance in social systems all around the world of "change agents," the Peace Corps, radical organizers, and the like will clear aside some of the romantic notions surrounding such roles and pave the way for a rational analytic of structural change. One of the first tasks of a rational "change agent" would be to obtain measures of the characteristics of the target system. In many cases it will be possible to develop applications in the framework of a clear map of structural potential so, for example, rural cooperatives, migrant labor specialists, or community schools could be located in areas that are ready for them (i.e., already developed enough in other ways to provide a good foundation for innovative programming). This approach would permit the "change agent" to establish a structural baseline for program evaluation. From the standpoint of such a baseline, some communities will appear to develop themselves. In them, the addition of a clinic or other program is a routine structural adjustment that occurs more or less automatically. This would be the case, for example, in a community with a complete set of institutions and services leading up to a clinic, and with solidarity and centrality racing ahead of differentiation. In other communities, not so structurally ready for institutional growth, the addition of a clinic would be a sign of Herculean effort and would also be a real risk in terms of its staying power.

In short, macrosocial accounting takes some of the magic out of community work and provides a basis for a true assessment of community change efforts. Obviously change is not change for its own sake, and my colleague Don Voth provides the bridge from change theory to action.

BIBLIOGRAPHY AND REFERENCES

Durkheim, Emile *The Rules of Sociological Method* 8th Ed. translated by Sarah Solovay & John Muller ed. G. Callin Glencoe Ill. The Free Press, 1950.

MacCannell, D. Negative solidarity. *Human Organization* (in press).

Redfield, Robert *The Folk Culture of Yucatan* Chicago, Ill. The Chicago University Press, 1950.

Spencer, B. Community differentiation and the fallacy of intersectoral causation. *Human Organization,* 1973, **32,** 59–71.

Wheelock, G. & Young, F. Macrosocial accounting for municipalities in the philippines. *Cornell International Agricultural Bulletin,* Number 26, 1973.

Young, F. Location and reputation in a Mexican intervillage network. *Human Organization,* 1964, **23,** 36–41.

Young, F. & Fujimoto, I. Social differentiation in Latin American communities. *Economic Development and Cultural Change,* 1965, **13:**344–352.

Young, F. & Young, R. C. Comparative studies of community growth. *Rural Sociological Society Monograph 2.* Morgantown, W. Va.: West Virginia University Press, 1973.

Young, R. C., The structural context of Caribbean agricultural: A comparative study. *Journal of Developing Areas,* 1976, **10**(4), 425–444.

Young, R. C. & Larson, O. The contribution of voluntary organizations to community structure. *The American Journal of Sociology.* 1965, **71** (2), 178–186.

Chapter 4

SOCIAL ACTION RESEARCH IN COMMUNITY DEVELOPMENT
Donald E. Voth

INTRODUCTION

There is an uneasiness about the relationship between
community development and the traditional social
sciences. Part of that uneasiness is expressed by Dean Mac-
Cannell in Chapter 3. This uneasiness becomes most acute
when the question of the contribution that research can
make to community development arises. The conventional
wisdom has it that community development is, essentially,
a methodology, that community development practitioners
obtain the scientific generalizations on which their methods
are based from the social sciences, and that these generalizations are derived from social science research. Since
community development practitioners are trained in universities in, or very closely related to, social science departments, it is generally assumed that they should be familiar
with the research techniques used by the social sciences
and that, consequently, training in these research techniques should be an integral part of community development training.

There are times when one cannot help but wonder about this conventional wisdom. Several years of working with community development students on required research projects following this basic paradigm has caused me to wonder, specifically, about the role of research and research training in community development training. The cases where one feels confident that these research experiences contributed significantly to the skills required to work as community development practitioners are the exception, not the rule.

Action research, not as a particular research methodology, but as an approach to the relationship between research and action in group and community settings, may provide a more coherent frame of reference within which to deal with the issue of the role of research in community development training.

THE ORIGINS OF ACTION RESEARCH

The term "action research" has been used in a number of different disciplinary and institutional settings. It has been applied most consistently to research and consultation carried out by social scientists in formal organizational settings. As Rapoport (1970, p. 500) has pointed out, some of the earliest work that used this term was carried out by the Tavistock Institute in Human Relations in London. One of the earliest articles describing action research was written by Curle (1949). The work of the Tavistock Institute was characterized by a clinical and psychoanalytic frame of reference, and focused on the solution of problems of organizations instead of the scientific or academic pursuits of the professional social scientists involved. Another closely related development was the work of Kurt Lewin and his associates at the Massachusetts Institute of Technology, and later at the University of Michigan. This group was somewhat less applied in its orientation, had closer ties with experimental psychology, and focused somewhat more on the individual and his or her relationship to organization than the Tavistock group did.

Another source of interest in action research was found in applied anthropology—specifically the branch of applied anthropology that sought to apply anthropological methods and insights to formal organizational settings in complex societies. Mayo, Roethlesberger, Dixon, and Whyte are some of the names associated with these developments, and Whyte and Hamilton's book (1965) discusses the relationship of Whyte's work to that of the Tavistock group and other similar developments in the social science community.

It is noteworthy that another concurrent development in applied anthropology, the use of professional anthropologists in the task of developing and integrating underdeveloped communities into larger national societies—community development—did not adopt the concept of action research as a unique research strategy.

Thus the earliest uses of the term action research are associated almost entirely with work in formal organizational settings where, typically, social scientists are brought in to assist in solving relatively clearly identified problems for relatively clearly defined clients by drawing on their expertise in psychology, social psychology, and organizational analysis. This expertise is applied in an "on the job" research and consultation process. There is some disagreement about the proper balance between applied objectives and the objective of contributing to social science theory and research. On the whole, however, the latter has played a very significant role in action research in the settings discussed above. In some cases action research is done primarily to contribute to scientific knowledge, and the action research strategy is selected simply because it is the most appropriate way to study organizational change.

What relationship does this intellectual tradition have to community development? That both work with groups is obvious; that, to some extent, both are concerned with the development of some kind of community among persons involved as targets or community members is equally obvious. Furthermore, those who work in this tradition frequently use the term "community" to refer to their target groups. For example, Curle, in defining the aims of action research, states: "[Action research] aims not only to discover facts, but to help in altering certain conditions experienced by the community as unsatisfactory" (Curle, 1949). Also, it is frequently suggested that the techniques used in these more clearly defined client-consultant situations can be applied to communities at large (Rappoport, 1970, pp. 509–510). Although the suggestion has a certain attractiveness, attributed to by the popularity of the Lippett, Watson, and Westley textbook (1958) among community development practitioners there are many who feel that the client-consultant paradigm does not fit most community development situations.

Thus the relevance for community development is not so much the theoretical orientation or the research technique, but the peculiar relationship between research and action within an ongoing community that is relevant.

The term action research has also been used in the social work literature, where it refers to various types of community self-studies or studies of community facilities and needs. Carter (1959, pp. 194–200) has discussed action research in a short but useful paper. Several of her "principles" illustrate the characteristics that distinguish action research in this context.

> *Principle Number 1.* The problem for research should stem from a recognized community need rather than (an) hypothesis generated from the personal interest of the research specialist.
> *Principle Number 2.* For maximum effectiveness, those who

are expected to implement the recommendations should participate in the study process.

Principle Number 6. Action research in community planning implies teamwork among researchers, other professionals, technicians, and lay citizenry.

Principle Number 7. The motivations for action research effect the nature of the research as well as its utilization.

Principle Number 8. An action research project should result in recommendations for action or social change. (pp. 195–200)

In this environment the psychological and social-psychological orientation and the client-consultant relationship are not so prominent; the research is more likely to be "objective," involving the analysis of community health and welfare facilities, financial needs in health and welfare institutions, and so forth. However, the relationship between research and action remains the same. Significant elements of the community are intimately involved in the research process, and the research is performed to inform and enlighten the community and to stimulate some kind of action program on the part of the community.

There has been one attempt to apply the action research framework directly to community development (Schler, 1967). Schler's objectives are ambitious.

> In this paper we are suggesting a new perspective on action research which stems from combining its methodology with the theory, philosophy and approach of community development to conscious, deliberate, planned change. The combination of the elements and components of community development and action research are seen to provide an ethical and effective means for the establishment of a new set of criteria by which decision making can occur and likewise provide an opportunity for the creation of various systems through which concerned decision making may take place at various levels of society. (p. 2)

Schler then identifies a series of principles of action research that are very similar to those of Carter. Some major points that are emphasized are that action research is a cooperative effort of community people and research professionals, that all significant elements of the community should be involved, and that the goal should be rational planning, programming, and decision making in the community. He especially emphasizes the participatory aspects of action research.

Several characteristics stand out in these treatments of action research: (1) action research involves a client organization, or a community on the one hand and social science or community development practitioners or professionals located in a sponsoring agency on the other, (2) participation of elements of the client organization or of the community is essential to the action research process, because they define the problems and act on the information provided by the research, and (3) a partipatory, democratic organization or community is one of the major objectives of the research.

A Definition of Action Research for Community Development

With this background, I propose the following definition of action research: "Action research is research used as a tool or technique, an integral part of the community or organization in all aspects of the research process, and has as its objectives the acquisition of valid information, action, and the enhancement of the problem solving capabilities of the community or organization."

Some examples will help to clarify this definition. The research process of the "self-study" style of community development (Bruyn, 1963) is action research, since research is one of the many techniques used—together with public meetings, use of media, and various kinds of committees—in achieving community development. On the

other hand, impact evaluation (Suchman, 1967) is not necessarily action research, since it attempts to stand outside
the community development process in order to observe,
analyze, and evaluate that process. So-called "process evaluation" (Suchman, 1967), which provides ongoing feedback while an action program is in effect, may be action
research, since it is also an integral part of the action process.

There are many research activities using this definition
that may be used in action research—various kinds of "ad-
vocacy" research, much of what is referred to as "community research" by radical movement groups (Jones,
Cheever, & Ficklin, 1971), the self-study style of community development (Bruyn, 1963; Poston, 1953; Sanders,
1953; Warren, 1963), systematic recording of program inputs and outputs, and many others.

The distinctive feature is not a particular methodology, but the relationship that the research activity has to
community development and to the people who are part of
the community development process. Action research provides some kind of valid information or intelligence that is
required for the community development process to occur.
It involves the community itself in obtaining this intelligence and in acting on it. This intelligence may be feedback
on the community development process and its progress or
lack of it (process evaluation), or it may be essential data
about the environment in which the process occurs (economic base studies, etc.); in any case, it involves a process
of education, self-education, or enlightenment, which the
community development process requires of its participants.

Action research, defined in this way, is a key element
in community development in most of its forms, in that
community development almost always involves a commitment to problem solving and decision making *with* people
instead of *for* them. It is also an important element in the

continued viability of our political systems, both in industrialized and in unindustrialized countries. For a long time a combination of pluralist and elitist interpretations of the actual functioning of the American political system have been the most widely accepted interpretations, and they have been regarded as contributing to system stability. As long as secondary groups were regarded as mediators between the citizen and the state, this interpretation was tolerable. However, it is becoming increasingly clear that these organizations serve the mediating function poorly, at best, that they are not democratic, that participation in them is highly dependent on social class and, in mass society, that people tend toward an extremely private existence. This results in alienation from the political system in which the citizen is very poorly informed about public issues; this in turn results in a volatile political system in that strong emotional appeals may bring these uninformed citizens out to vote irrationally.

Citizens and community groups, on the other hand, are concerned about how they can regain control of vast and complicated bureaucracies that, from their point of view, are almost entirely unaccountable to them.

In unindustrialized countries the problem is one of mobilizing the citizenry to participate in national development goals and objectives. Support for these goals and participation in them is essential for them to be achieved but, in many of these countries, there is a low level of identification with the nation for a variety of reasons, including the colonial experience, ethnic, linguistic, and regional conflicts, and a general lack of confidence in government.

Community development arose as a movement in this country and in underdeveloped countries primarily in response to these problems. It arose in university settings (Brownell, 1950; Bruyn, 1963; Poston, 1953); in the Cooperative Extension, in underdeveloped countries, and much more recently in the "Grey Areas" programs of the Ford Foundation and subsequently in Mobilization for Youth (Weissman, 1969) and the Office of Economic Opportunity. At the core, its answer to these concerns has always been the same radical idea, an idea that is very similar to Paulo Friere's "development of critical consciousness" *(conscientizacao)* (Friere, 1973). Its goal has always been helping community people to become subjects instead of objects, acting on their community situation instead of simply reacting. It places great faith in the rational capabilities of community people. Methodologically, it has involved the engagement of relatively small communities of people in the process of studying their own immediate situation as a community, deciding themselves what to do about it through a democratic procedure, carrying out their programs, evaluating their performace and, hopefully, developing, through the process, the ability to solve community problems efficiently and effectively. No doubt it is a utopian vision and no doubt many attempts to achieve it have been a caricature of the vision, but it is a vision that we desperately need to realize if the citizenry is to deal intelligently with the complex problems of an industrial society that is undergoing dramatic change.

What is involved, essentially, is community people making a transition from being objects of the polity, manipulated by the bureaucracy, adapting themselves to it, and so forth, to becoming subjects who consider issues, make decisions, and act responsibly vis-à-vis their community (Friere, 1973, pp. 4–5). To be sure, some advocates of community development have been reluctant to recognize the turmoil and conflict that such a process might entail and, consequently, have attempted to stimulate it at a very superficial level. Also, there has been a considerable amount of rural and small-town mythology involved in this vision. However, in one form or another, this radical view of community development persists, and it is, in my view, its single most valuable contribution.

But carrying out this idea requires a special kind of research process, a process that actively engages the citizenry in studying and analyzing the community, not merely in order to co-opt the people into supporting a course of action, not merely in order to "educate," "dealienate," or "deapathize" the citizens, but to place the responsibility for decision making squarely on them.

This research process is action research. Placing it in this context makes its value commitments explicit and identifies its basic goals and objectives.

ACTION RESEARCH AND COMMUNITY DEVELOPMENT TRAINING

There are problems with doing, not to mention teaching, action research defined in this way. The major type of action research that has been carried out by community developers is the "self-study" style of community development. No doubt it has successfully achieved many different objectives. However, there has been very little careful effort to evaluate it from the point of view of its contribution to civic education or its "process" objectives (Voth, 1975). Indeed, careful case studies suggest that in some instances the rhetoric of community involvement and decision making has been used to mask a very elitist process (Richmond, 1974).

Some of my own research in southern Illinois is relevant to this point. Out of 29 communities that had self-study community development programs and 32 control communities, although there had been some improvement in program communities in some aspects of community infrastructure, there had been no improvement in levels of voting participation. There was some improvement in the numbers of people competing for local offices. The latter should probably be regarded as elite participation and, as such, is not necessarily an action research goal. Unfortunately, I was not able to measure the more subtle aspects of citizen involvement and education (Voth, 1975).

Economic opportunity programs and model cities programs have both involved action research activities, and there is a growing literature on the relative success of these approaches, much of which does pay attention to citizen involvement in the research and planning process and the effects that this has had on the citizenry (Office of Community Development, 1973; Vanecko et al., 1970). What we know almost nothing about are the characteristics and skills of the people who have been the most successful in stimulating and facilitating this process, and this is what we need to know to begin to discuss the training of action research skills.

There are other problems involved in doing and teaching action research. Its primary characteristic is the integration of research, action, and participation. However, the institutional environments within which most of us work have long and firmly held traditions that separate action and research and, to make matters worse, that separate out a third function and call it teaching. In the land grant institutions the separation of research, teaching, and extension, in which extension insists on avoiding the action phases of the very processes that it may stimulate (through County Development Committees or Councils, etc.) frustrates carrying out action research in the true sense of the term. This separation also creates difficulties for training community development practitioners in general because of the need o integrate practice and learning in such training. If opportunities are not available for students to work in real-world situations, integrating what they learn in the classroom, community development training is severely hampered.

In nonland grant institutions the problems of inadequate financing and the accountability movement threaten to eliminate or seriously hamper institutional commitments to services and research, through which faculties can have an authentic involvement in action research and, more particularly, through which students can be given practical field experiences.

Finally, there are problems with staffing community development training programs. Those who successfully pursue community development as practitioners frequently do not have the formal credentials to get into the university to start with and, if they are there, their status is insecure. On the other hand, those who have the academic credentials frequently are short on field experience, having devoted their time getting a Ph.D. which, normally, also means devoting themselves to a more or less pure science research paradigm and not getting much field experience.

One should, at some point, attempt to identify the skills that are required to do action research and comment on how they can be obtained. However, we really know very little about this, except for the obvious: that excellence should be sought in general research capabilities, that persons should be skilled in problem solving with people, that they should have an understanding of organizations and organizational dynamics, public administration, business management, and the like. Obviously one cannot hope to be proficient in all of these areas, so the typical community development student will probably want to select a set of skills that he or she feels most comfortable with or thinks will be most useful to—including skills in problem solving with people. Indeed, the crucial element from the point of view of action research is the ability to integrate formal skills of many kinds with the ability to engage in problem analysis and solution with community people. This can only be learned in real-world situations: in internships, in apprenticeship relationships with skilled community developers, or on the job after completing formal educational requirements. Internships and apprenticeships as models for training community developers may fall on hard times because of budget squeezes, the accountability movement, and the separation of action, research, and teaching in universities. Whatever the situation, and it surely varies from place to place, I believe we should at least consider a different model than the one most commonly used. Perhaps what we should try to do is integrate classroom work, in the form of relatively short, intensive seminars, into a fairly long series of full-time work experiences that the students obtain for themselves, but following a general program and under the supervision of a community development practitioner who has one foot in practice and one in teaching and research. The students would not receive their degrees or accreditation until they had worked in a variety of settings that would allow them to integrate substantive and research skills into action settings, and simultaneously provide feedback to the sponsoring educational institution on what classroom training was useful and what was not. To do this we need much more flexibility, both in the university and in the world of work, so that the walls between the two are more permeable.

Whatever is done, we need a better picture of the role that research plays in community development practice, and training programs need to be designed to facilitate that role instead of continuing to be adopted from a traditional social science pattern that may or may not be applicable. Edward Alchin and Pairat Decharin offer a quasipractitioner approach to this dilemma next.

BIBLIOGRAPHY AND REFERENCES

Brownell, B. *The human community.* New York: Harper & Bros., 1950.

Bruyn, S. T. *Communities in action: Pattern and process.* New Haven, Conn.: College and University Press, 1963.

Carter, G. W. Action research. In Ernest B. Harper and Arthur Dunham (Eds.), *Community organization in action: Basic literature and critical comments.* New York: Association Press, 1959. Pp. 194–200.

Clark, A. W. Sanction, a critical element in action research. *The Journal of Applied Behavioral Science,* 1972, **8,** 713–731.

Curle, A. A theoretical approach to action research. *Human Relations,* **2,** 269–280.

Friere, P. *Pedagogy of the oppressed.* New York: Herder and Herder, 1970.

Friere, P. *Education for critical consciousness.* New York: The Seabury Press, 1973.

Jones, W. R., Cheever, J., & Ficklin, J. *Finding community: A guide to community research and action,* Palo Alto, Calif.: James E. Freel & Associates, 1971.

Klein, D. E., Sensitivity training and community development. In Edgar H. Schein and Waren G. Bennis (Eds.) *Personal and organizational change Through group methods.* New York: John Wiley & Sons, 1965.

Lippett, R., Watson, J., & Westley, B. *The dynamics of planned change: A comparative study of planned change.* New York: Harcourt, Brace, 1958.

Office of Community Development, Evaluation Division, Department of Housing and Urban Development. *The Model Cities Program: A Comparative Analysis of City Response Patterns and Their Relation to Future Urban Policy.* Washington, D.C.: U.S. Government Printing Office, 1975.

Poston, R. *Democracy is you.* New York: Harper & Row, 1953.

Rappoport, R. N., Three dilemmas in action research. *Human Relations,* 1970, **23,** 499–513.

Richmond, L. Active community thought: Myth and reality of a community development program. Unpublished masters thesis, Southern Illinois University, 1974.

Sanders, I. T. *Making good communities better.* Lexington, Ky.: University of Kentucky Press, 1953.

Schler, D. The current status of action research. Item Number 24 of *Readings in the Theory and Practice of Community Development,* Columbia, Mo., Department of Regional and Community Affairs, 1967.

Suchman, E. A. *Evaluative research: Principles and practice in public service and social action programs.* New York: Russell Sage, 1967.

Vanecko, J. J., Orden, S. R., & Hoolander, S. *Community organization efforts, political and institutional change, and the diffusion of change produced by community action programs.* Chicago: National Opinion Research Center (NORC), University of Chicago, 1970.

Voth, D. E., An evaluation of community development programs in Illinois. *Social Forces,* 1975.

Voth, D. E. An evaluation of community development programs in Illinois. *Social Forces,* 1975.

Warren, R. L. *The community in America.* Chicago: Rand McNally, 1963.

Weissman, H. D. *Community development in the mobilization for youth experience.* New York: Association Press, 1969.

Whyte, W. F., & Hamilton, E. L. *Action research for management.* Homewood, Ill.: Richard Irwin, 1965.

Chapter 5

AN ECOSYSTEMS APPROACH TO COMMUNITY DEVELOPMENT RESEARCH

Edmond W. Alchin and Pairat Decharin

INTRODUCTION

The initial contact between community leaders and community development practitioners to explore problems and needs usually results in general agreement of program objectives. There remains a need to examine and refine program goals, so a wide range of information must be obtained, organized, and prepared by the community development staff. The information needed is that which is required to identify specific development needs, to determine feasible alternatives for projects, and to plan a program and organize leaders to accomplish it—in short, to establish program priorities and carry out the community action process.

Metropolitan areas and cities of 50,000 or more population contain many public and private agencies, boards, commissions, and associations that employ professionals to obtain and analyze data and recommend plans for development effort. Usually the role of the community development practitioner in this setting is to act as facilitator and coordinator of plans to assist local managers to optimize benefits of development efforts. However, in agricultural areas and smaller cities and villages, there are fewer professional experts available, and they have responsibilities for countywide or regional assistance to local municipalities. In this situation the community development practitioner must take on much more of the responsibility for obtaining and utilizing information needed.

The following plan is designed to provide a framework and guidelines for practical research to be carried out within a community to provide the data and information needed. The plan suggests a diagnostic procedure to be conducted by the staff of a community development organization in the early stages of contact with the community. The plan combines ideas from matrix and systems analysis and is based on standard procedures from a number of disciplines for obtaining, organizing, and presenting quantitative and qualitative data.

OBJECTIVES AND ASSUMPTIONS

The objectives for the plan are:

1. *To provide reliable indicators of the potential for development* from the standpoint of resources available and to furnish insights as to existing and future plans for physical, economic, political, and other social development programs.
2. *To initiate a systematic procedure for gathering data* to determine the existing basis for the dynamics of community action.
3. *To provide guidelines to additional research* in relation to both the planning and execution of the commu-

nity action and to opportunities to add to the body of knowledge concerning community development.

The foundation for this research plan is based on several assumptions concerning community development and the role of the community development practitioners.

1. Community is defined as the place where decisions can be made and action can be implemented to achieve development goals.
2. Community development is concerned with bringing about changes in organizations, objectives, plans, and behavior of people.
3. The ultimate goal of community development is to improve availability, distribution, and utilization of resources to provide the necessities (needs) and culturally determined imperatives (desires, wants, and wishes) of the people of the community.
4. Information is a critical need for the community development process. That information includes:
    a. The kind and amount of resources available.
    b. Means to improve the preparation, availability, and utilization of resources.
    c. Present and future plans and activities for obtaining, preparing, distributing, and utilizing resources.
5. As agents of change, community development practitioners intercede in an ongoing process of planning and action to introduce ideas that affect existing and future plans of the people and organizations in the community.
6. Participation of leaders and citizens in the identification of problems and needs and in the planning and carrying out of development programs is essential.

Conceptual Framework

Based on the foregoing objectives for the research effort and the assumptions concerning the community development process, the conceptual framework for the plan combines an ecosystem model of community, an input-output model of development, and a plan for a selective attitude survey. These models collectively provide the desired guidelines to needed data, suggest a means for organizing and relating information, and outline procedures for gathering the data.

Community Ecosystem

The ecosystem model views a community as consisting of a population in a geographic area made up of a human component as the principal organic system and the manufactured and natural components as the environmental systems (see Figure 5–1).

Figure 5-1   The community ecosystem.

Components	Description
Human	The population of a geographic area, the social structure, organizations, and interaction among individuals and organizations
Manmade	The buildings and other structures, machines, tools, materials and artifacts
Natural	The land, water, minerals, petroleum, climate and other organic systems

The human component of the community ecosystem has the capacity to develop rationally social organizations and institutions; to develop, store, and transmit a body of knowledge from one generation to the next; and to invent, build, organize, and manage structures, machines, and tools in order to obtain, prepare, distribute, and utilize resources.

The physical structures, machines, tools, and materials that people build and manage are the manufactured component. They are identifiable and can be described quantitatively and qualitatively. They can be classified in terms of their relationship to the social, economic, political, educational, and religious units of organization of the human component.

The natural component provides the space, food, and materials to sustain the human component and materials with which the human component creates the manufactured component.

COMMUNITY CHARACTERISTICS

An understanding of the characteristics of the components of the community ecosystem is essential to the determination of specific goals for development. The characteristics of the components can be determined, quantified, and/or described using standard methods and procedures of related disciplines. Figure 5–2 presents a way of viewing components that provides the means for accommodating the needed materials and procedures.

The information required (as suggested in Figure 5–2) is contained in secondary sources such as census reports or is a matter of record that is easily available in offices of related organizations in the community. The model does suggest the need for inputs by demographers, economists, political analysts, educators, urban planners, and a number

Figure 5-2 Community characteristics.

	Human component				
Social	Economic	Political	Educational	Religious
Population change	Production	Prevailing philosophy	Level of attainment	Doctrine(s)
Population characteristics	Distribution	Government form	Kind available	Denominations
Social structure	Finance	Government structure	Curriculum	Participation
Social organization	Labor force	Public services	Enrollment	Community services
Health	Employment	Government finance	Finance	
Welfare	Income	Legislative body	Community service	
Arts and crafts	Communications	Judicial		
Leisure-recreation	Transportations	Protective agencies		
Attitudes	Energy	Voting habits		

Manmade component

The level of technology. The kind, number, size or capacity, condition, age, and the location of structures, their functions (or by-function), and their interrelationship

Natural component

The kind, amount, location, classification or quality, and present use(s) of land, water, minerals, energy, climate, and domesticated and wild organic systems of natural scientists. However, for the most part and for most communities, much of the work of these specialists has already been done and is available.

COMMUNITY SYSTEMS

Another set of information useful to the plan for systems research is the identification of the organizations that must be concerned with development action.

Figure 5–3 indicates a way of classifying units of community organization that are important to achieve developmental goals. The units of organization are viewed as social systems that can be identified and classified using methods and procedures suggested by social science and natural science disciplines.

The systems that the human component develops and manages receive inputs of resources that are converted to outputs of goods and services that are, in turn, distributed for consumption. These systems are interdependent and are interrelated through links that form a network within a community ecosystem (see Figure 5–4).

The resource input into community systems can be classified as:

1. *Materials.* Organic and inorganic substances, machines, and tools.
2. *Energy.* Chemical, electrical, mechanical, thermonuclear, and so forth.
3. *People.* Management and labor.
4. *Information.* The knowledge needed to invent, build, manage, and operate systems.

The output of systems is culturally determined and limited by availability of resources and technological skill.

Figure 5-3 Systems of the community ecosystem.

Social	Economic	Political	Educational	Religious
Community associations	Manufacturing units	Party organizations	K-12 districts	Churches by doctrine
Ethnic organizations	Agriculture related	Executive units	Parochial units	Churches by denomination
Racial organizations	Extractive units	Legislative units	Community college	Professional associations
Health service	Wholesale units	Administrative units	Colleges and universities	Lay bodies or associations
Welfare service	Retail units	Protective units	Trade schools	
Service clubs	Banking and finance	Judicial units	Vocational training	
Older persons	Communications	Penal units	Associations	
Youth associations	Transportation	Associations		
Womens associations	Domestic services			
Recreation-leisure associations	Recreation services			
Fine arts organizations	Energy units			
Professional associations	Labor associations			
	Other associations			

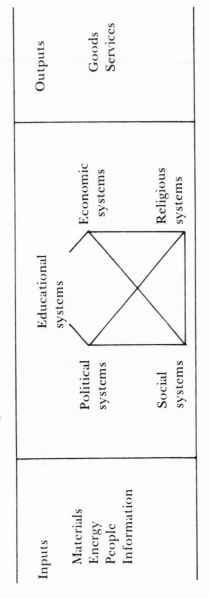

Figure 5-4   The function of community systems.

Within their limits, the outputs of goods and services are those that the human component values in terms of social, economic, and psychological satisfaction.

Effective community development programs require a change in the kind, amount, availability, and/or distribution of goods and services within a community. This, in turn, requires changing the management and/or relationships of community systems. The The community development professional needs to identify the dynamics of the community systems that will have to change if development goals are to be achieved. The following suggests a procedure for meeting this need.

Community systems have elements that provide the means of converting resources to goods and services.

1. *Channels or paths* through which resources move over time.
2. Control points where:
   a. *Transactions* take place (negotiation and agreement to exchange resources).
   b. *Storage* takes place (resources are stored for future use).
   c. Conversion takes place (resources are converted from one state to another).
   d. *Distribution* takes place (resources are routed for further storage or conversion, or goods and services are routed for transaction and consumption).
3. *Linkages* are rerouting points where resources and/or goods and services are transferred from one channel to another or from one system to another.
4. *Control people* who:
   a. Carry on transactions to obtain resources.
   b. Make management decisions concerning storage, conversion, or distribution within the system.

   c. Make management decisions concerning linkages and flow of resources to other systems inside and outside the community.

   The systems' control points delineate the community
for community development purposes. Communities can
be viewed as a hierarchy of ecosystems reaching from family to local unit of government, to county, to state and
national, and even to world levels, depending on the nature
of the development program.

DECISION-MAKING PROCESS

In order to plan an effective community development
effort, it is critically important to understand the decision-
making process of controllers of community systems.
   The model that provides the guidelines for research
into the decision-making process is based on the idea that
individuals have *images,* or a perception, understanding,
and interpretation of the world around them. Images are
culturally determined and are composed of values, beliefs,
traditions, and mores—the collective knowledge and wisdom of the individual—and can be shared or not shared.
Images result in plans. *Plans* are sets of instructions for
individual, group, or community behavior. Plans can be
unwritten, socially determined or written blueprints for
action. Action is the execution or implementation of plans.
Each step in the process of converting *images* to *action* involves *evaluation.* Evaluation is the process of determining
objectives and alternatives, discussion, negotiation, compromise, decision, and transactions to achieve individual
and/or group goals. These processes can be called the
I-P-A-E of the individual and are represented diagrammati-
cally in Figure 5–5.

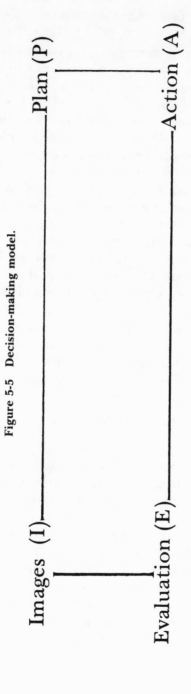

Figure 5-5   Decision-making model.

Within the community ecosystem, the images and plans in various systems are sometimes shared within the system and sometimes not, are sometimes shared outside the system and sometimes not, and are sometimes shared with the community as a whole and sometimes not.

As images and plans are evaluated and converted into action, new images and new plans emerge. The process is cyclic, ongoing, and never-ending.

The community development practitioner is a change agent of a change system. He or she also has images of and plans for the development possibilities within the community ecosystem. These images and plans should be expected to be more holistic and more sophisticated than those of community leaders. The goal of the community development practitioner is to make a plan, to obtain and disseminate information based on an understanding of the community ecosystem and the images and plans of control people in the system. The community development plan should form a bridge between existing images and plans and the possibilities for improving development.

IMPLICATION OF THE FRAMEWORK

The foregoing theoretical framework provides conceptual models for determining the characteristics of community components, identifying and classifying systems of the community, identifying leaders of the community, and gaining insight into the dynamics of community decision making. However, the models suggest only generally the information that must be supplied. The community development practitioner must develop the detailed plan for obtaining the information to be gathered. It is suggested that a working manual with a checklist for the desired detailed data be developed using guidelines provided by the models that make up the framework and developed with the help of specialists from the appropriate disciplines.

Procedures to Implement the Plan

Procedures have been developed to carry out the activities necessary to obtain, organize, and analyze the information suggested by the models that make up the conceptual framework. The plan was developed and tested in several Michigan communities and in a countywide pilot program. The procedures consist of the following interdependent sets of activities.

1. *Collect and review existing studies,* surveys, reports, maps, directories, and news accounts of current and recent development activities. These include planning studies, economic base surveys, school studies, public service and utilities studies, financial reports of banks and other financial institutions and industries, fiscal plans and budgets of public agencies, and soil and geodetic surveys.

2. *Extract and study data from secondary sources* where this has not been done by competent specialists. Such sources include data from census reports on population, economic base, and the like, health statistics, departments of education, labor agencies, and social welfare agencies. Where appropriate, compile and analyze data on population change and characteristics, level of education, economic base, employment, income, wholesale and retail trade, health conditions, poverty and welfare, land use and characteristics, and natural resources.

3. *Make systematic observations of the community* and the nearby area to gain insight into the nature and characteristics of the human, manufactured, and natural components and the major institutions and systems of the community. Note the probable influence of the systems identified on community

affairs, the nature of the control points located in the community, and the resources used and goods or services provided by the systems. Try to delineate the functional boundary of the community and identify probable regional influences affecting the municipality.

4. *Select and interview key informants* to determine their images of community needs and problems, plans for the development of the community ecosystem, and how they think things should be done. Based on the interviews, consider organization and communications probabilities and conflict that can be expected. The key informants are the persons in control points of important systems that have been identified in the observations made of the community. They include the people responsible for the management of important physical, economic, political, educational, and religious systems of the community and leaders of ethnic, racial, and service associations.

PERSONNEL REQUIRED

Many of the activities required in carrying out the procedures to implement the action research plan can be done by the community development practitioner. The practitioner or generalist can collect and summarize studies and reports, make systematic observations of the community, and identify and interview key informants. The extraction, organization, and analysis of data from secondary sources, however, usually requires the attention of a specialist schooled in the appropriate subject matter. As noted in the introduction, specialists are usually available within metropolitan areas and larger cities. Although not usually available in smaller cities, villages, and rural areas, county and regional level agencies and associations do have specialists in a number of important fields. These specialists generally are responsible for providing needed assistance or are available on a low-cost contract basis to local government officials and agencies. When local professionals are not available, it is often possible to obtain specialists' help from local school systems, community colleges, and state colleges and universities (particularly land grant institutions).

SPECIFIC INFORMATION PROVIDED

The data, insights, and understandings provided by the initial research efforts—the review of existing studies and reports, the compilation and analysis of data from secondary sources and the observations of the community—include the following.

Key Informant Interviews

The key informant interviews are a unique feature of the action research plan. This part of the plan provides insights into the dynamics of community interaction and decision making, the roles of individuals and systems, and the way people relate to each other in the community development process.

THE SELECTION OF KEY INFORMANTS.   The selection of key informants is basically an exercise in identifying middle- and upper-level power figures in the community ecosystem. It is assumed that the key informants will be those who control inputs and outputs of resources and manage systems. They include (1) executives and managers, (2) professionals who manage institutions, and (3) officers of associations.

Selection of the key informants depends on the judgment of the community development practitioner and is largely a matter of deciding who may be key people in providing information that will be useful in future interviews. The judgments of the practitioner are based on the findings of the studies and observations that have been carried out.

As interviews progress, each informant is asked to provide names of people who should be interviewed and also names of people who do not agree with some of his or her ideas. In this way, opposition informants and issues of conflict are identified.

"Checkoff informants" are also selected, at random, to test the extent to which the images and plans of control people are understood and accepted in the community. This group should include old-timers, newcomers, youth leaders, and housewives. The interviews with checkoff informants also serve to relate images and plans to the characteristics of the population.

CONDUCTING AND OBJECTIVES OF INTERVIEWS.   For purposes of conducting the interviews, lead questions—which relate to specific images that the informants have of important aspects of the community with respect to development possibilities—form the basis for further questions. Examples of lead questions include: What are the important changes that have taken place in recent years? What activities are helping development at the present time? Who are the people and organizations getting things done? Who could be of more help? What are some of the priorities for development in the future? How will resources be obtained to get the job done? What changes in attitudes and cooperation will be necessary to get the job done?

The general objective of the key informant interview is to determine the unshared (individual's personal) and shared (interest group and community) images and plans.

Specifically, the objective of these interviews is to obtain from the informants their images and/or plans vis à vis the same characteristics and dynamics of the community ecosystem extrapolated from the studies and reports, namely, important historical events, community boundaries, component characteristics, community systems and their elements, and the inputs and outputs of resources.

IMPORTANT VARIABLES TO CONSIDER.   Within the framework of the specific areas of inquiry outlined above, several critical variables are essential to achieving the objectives of the action research plan. They form the basis for the structuring of lead questions and probes. The variables are:

1. *Social Values.* The philosophical and moral basis for the informant's images; that is, why the informant believes what he or she does.
2. *Social Organization and Social Structure.* The informant's perception of organizations and individuals, their objectives and status relationships, and how the informant sees his or her position and role.
3. *Institutionalization.* How change becomes accepted; that is, how individuals change images, how organizations change objectives, and how new relationships to other organizations and new organizations emerge in the community ecosystem.
4. *Conflict.* Individual, intergroup, and intercommunity conflict that must be neutralized or can be turned to advantage in bringing about change.
5. *Time Allocation.* Reallocation of the time that individuals and groups commit to various activities as change takes place.
6. *Information.* The amount, kind, and source of information available, and the way information flows in the community.

7. *The Planning Process and Network Planning.* How plans are formed, the flow of events, who is involved, and how objectives are achieved.

SUMMARY AND CONCLUSION

The ecosystem approach integrates the concept of the community as a unit with a "holistic" research strategy. The community, its people, and natural and physical resources are assessed systematically through the prism of their own design. This approach yields both soft and hard data. The soft information is contained in the observed views, perceptions, and attitudes of the people in the system. The hard data come from the system description. Merging both of these into a research plan and, subsequently, into action is what community development is all about. Thus the research strategy in this technique forms the core of the strategy for action.

In the ensuing chapter Ed Blakely and Howard Schutz lay out more specifically how this method might be adopted for policy planning purposes.

BIBLIOGRAPHY AND REFERENCES

Books

Arensberg, C., & Kimball, S. T. *Culture and community.* New York: Harcourt, Brace and World, 1965.

Babbie, E. R. *Survey research methods.* Belmont, Calif.: Wadsworth Publishing, 1973.

Batten, T. R. *Training for community development.* London: Oxford University Press, 1962.

Beal, G. M., Powers, R., & Coward, Jr., E. W. (Eds.) *Sociological perspectives of domestic development.* Ames, Ia.: Iowa State University Press, 1971.

Bell, C., & Newby, H. *Community studies: An introduction to the sociology of the local community.* New York: Praeger Publishers, 1972.

Bernard, J. *The sociology of community.* Glenview, Ill.: Scott, Foresman, 1973.

Boulding, K. E. *The image.* Ann Arbor, Mich.: University of Michigan Press, 1956.

Brager, G., & Specht, H. *Community organizing.* New York: Columbia University Press, 1973.

Carey, L. J. (Ed.) *Community development as a process.* Columbia, Mo.: University of Missouri Press, 1970.

Caro, F. G. (Ed.) *Readings in evaluation research.* New York: Russell Sage Foundation, 1971.

Chodak, S. *Societal development.* New York: Oxford University Press, 1973.

Cox, F. M., Erlich, J. L., Rothman, J., & Trapman, J. E. (Eds.) *Strategies of community organization: A book of readings.* Itasca, Ill.: F. E. Peacock Publishers, 1978.

Ewald, W., Jr. (Ed.) *Environment for man: The next fifty years.* Bloomington, Ind. and London: Indiana University Press, 1967.

Filstead, W. J. (Ed.) *Qualitative methodology: Firsthand involvement with the social world.* Chicago, Ill.: Markham Publishing, 1970.

Forcese, D. P., & Richer, S. (Eds.) Stages of social research: Contemporary perspectives. Englewood Cliffs, N.J.: Prentice-Hall, 1970.

French, R. M. (Ed.) *The community: A comparative perspective.* Itasca, Ill.: F. E. Peacock Publishers, 1969.

Goodman, W. I., & Freund, E. C. (Eds.) *Principles and practice of urban planning.* Washington, D.C.: International City Managers Association, 1968.

Hambridge, G. (Ed.) *Dynamics of development . . . An international development reader.* New York: Frederick A. Praeger, Publishers, 1964.

Havelock, R. G., & Havelock, M. C. *Training for change agents.* Ann Arbor, Mich.: Institute for Social Research, University of Michigan, 1973.

Hawley, W. D., & Wirt, F. M. (Eds.) *The search for community power.* Englewood Cliffs, N.J.: Prentice-Hall, 1968.

Hicks, H. G. *The management of organizations: A systems and human resources approach.* (2nd ed.) New York: McGraw-Hill, 1972.

Lassey, W. R. (Ed.) *Leadership and social change.* Iowa City, Ia.: University Associates Press, 1971.

Monane, J. H. *A sociology of human systems.* New York: Appleton-Century Crofts, 1967.

Phillips, B. S. *Social research: Strategy and tactics.* New York: The Macmillan Co., 1968.

Rothman, J. *Planning and organizing for social change.* New York: Columbia University Press, 1974.

Sanders, I. T. *The community: An introduction to a social system.* New York: Ronald Press, 1966.

Shields, J. J., Jr. *Education in community development.* New York: Frederick A. Praeger Publishers, 1967.

Suchman, E. A. *Evaluation research: Principles and practice in public service and social action programs.* New York: Russell Sage Foundation, 1967.

Warren, R. *Truth, love and social change.* Chicago: Rand McNally and Company, 1971.

Warren, R. *The community in America.* (2nd ed.) Chicago: Rand McNally and Company, 1972.

Warren, R. (Ed.) *Perspectives on the American community: A book of readings.* (2nd ed.) Chicago: Rand McNally and Company, 1973.

Weiss, C. H. *Evaluating action programs: Readings in social action and education.* Boston: Allyn and Bacon, Inc., 1972.

Articles, Bulletins and Papers

Alchin, E. W. Planned change: A practitioners model. (A mimeo paper), Institute for Community Development, Michigan State University, East Lansing, Michigan, 1962.

Alchin, E. W. *A holistic approach to community development.* Bulletin B41, Institute for Community Development, Michigan State University, East Lansing, Michigan, 1964.

Alchin, E. W. *A reconnaissance research plan for community development.* Bulletin B49, Institute for Community Development, Michigan State University, East Lansing, Michigan, 1966.

Anderson, R. C. Community cooperation and involvement. Institute for Community Development, Michigan State University, East Lansing, Michigan, 1968.

Beal, G. M., & Hobbs, D. J. *The process of social action in community and area development.* Cooperative Extension Service, Iowa State University, Ames, Iowa, 1964.

Biddle, W. W., & Dunham, A. *Currents in community development.* Department of Community Development, School of Social Work and Community Development, University of Missouri, Columbia, Missouri, 1964.

Duke, R. D. *Gaming simulation in urban research.* Monograph No. 23, Institute for Community Development, Michigan State University, East Lansing, Michigan, 1964.

Fessler, D. R. *Citizen participation in community development.* Bulletin 277, Extension Division, Virginia Polytechnic Institute, Blacksburg, Virginia, 1967.

King, G. W., Garber, S. K., & Brown, E. J. Organizational functions and linkages in resource development programs. A paper prepared for the Rural Sociological Society Meeting, Chicago, Illinois, 1965.

Marquis, S. *Communities and planning areas—A systems approach to spatial community.* Institute for Community Development, Michigan State University, East Lansing, Michigan, 1963.

Mezirow, J. D. Community development as an educational process. International Review of Community Development, No. 5, 1960.

Optner, S. L. Looking at the city as a system. Report to the Department of City Planning, City of Los Angeles, California, January 1959.

Pondy, L. R. Organizational conflict: Concepts and models. *Administrative Science Quarterly,* **12–2,** September 1967.

Sanders, I. T. Theories of Community Development. *Rural Sociology,* 1958, **23** (1).

VanMaanen, J. *The process of program evaluation.* National Tr. and Devel. Science Press, 5028 Wisc. Ave., N.W., Washington, D.C. 20016, 1973.

Wilkinson, K. P. Phases and roles in community action. *Rural Sociology,* 1970, **35** (1).

Chapter 6

A POLICY SYSTEMS APPROACH TO COMMUNITY DEVELOPMENT RESEARCH AND ACTION*

Edward J. Blakely and Howard Schutz

INTRODUCTION

Techniques for assessing community needs and translating this information into social policy form the core of the community development discipline. The earliest work in the field is based almost exclusively on the central concept of determining local individual and collective human needs and translating those desires into specific projects and programs (Biddle, 1965, Cary, 1970). Diagnostic activity in one form or another has dominated community development literature and remains the principle topic of current research efforts (Nix et al., 1965). However, in spite of the proliferation of community analysis techniques and technologies, there is a somewhat ominous feeling detected both in the current literature and at professional meetings

*Another version of this paper appeared in *Social Indicators Research,* 1977, **4,** 163–184.

that existing methods are inefficient, unworkable, or unreliable (Sargent, 1973). This issue is becoming critical, since both local city jurisdictions and the federal government are adopting the community development model or its rhetoric as the basis for current social policy in citizen participation, needs determination, formulation of social indicators, and evaluation of economic and social impact of federal programs (Eberts, 1975). In essence community development is replacing other social welfare methodologies such as economic development and social planning as the cornerstone of the public policy formulation process. However, at this juncture in the history of the community development profession, there is no codified or structured methodology for easy presentation to public policymakers. This unfortunate situation has led to recent attempts by other professionals (planners, engineers, social workers, city managers, and many others) "to reinvent the community diagnosis wheel." Regardless of whether there is "a" community development method or not, it seems apparent that there are forces at work prompting the community development profession to examine its current strategies and assess their utility in a rapidly changing community context. This chapter explores a systematic diagnostic and policy formulation strategy applicable to local city government. Our methodology is not put forward as a criticism of existing systems nor is it intended to be yet another alternative. It is our purpose to suggest that the *devolution* of federal and state authority of the New Federalism policies (revenue sharing, etc.) to the cities requires a systems-oriented community development methodology that addresses itself to the total process of policy development, implementation and monitoring of community economic, and physical and social development within the governance framework of the city. Furthermore, the community development policy for this purpose must be grounded in the context of current management or public economics to meet the latest governmental and popular criterion for *accountability*. It is our contention that current federal policy, local citizen sophistication, and the enormity of programs, policies, and regulation limit the utility and require the integration of the earlier community development models suggested by Batten, Poston, Warren, and others (Batten, 1957; Poston, 1962; Warren, 1968) into an integrated systems approach to be useful to city officials in urban and nonmetropolitan cities.

HISTORIC COMMUNITY DEVELOPMENT MODELS

Organizing the various community analysis methods into discrete categories or models is somewhat difficult and hazardous, since there is so much overlap among them. However, before we discuss integrative policy approaches, an inspection of the relevant literature is in order to examine some of the broad divisions in community development thought as it relates to the policy formulation process.

THE COMMUNITY INVENTORY TECHNIQUE

This is the oldest and most widely accepted method of determining community problems and assessing the existing resources in order to meet local needs. The technique pioneered by Poston, Biddle, Warren, and others involves citizen assessment of local conditions using some form of checklist or inventory document. Warren's excellent work, *Studying Your Community* (1968), remains the classic model using this approach. More recently, local governments have made adaptations of Warren's methods for the use of local administrative and elected officials.

Unfortunately, in highly complex urban environments this method appears too overwhelming (particularly following Warren's outline) to local officials, since there is such a plethora of community facilities and programs.

The Reconnaissance Approach

This approach resembles its name in that it describes a means of obtaining an overview or snapshot of a locale. Edmond Alchin and Pairat Decharin suggest this method in the previous chapter as a means to obtain significant amounts of data on a community or area quickly and relatively easily. The basic strategy in this method is to obtain key information from key citizens or interest groups by using a small sample of persons from each group. These data are compared with observations, secondary sources, and related information to formulate a fairly accurate picture of community needs and priorities.

This method provides good data on the community social systems, but it requires professional competence to use it effectively. Furthermore, this method is subject to professional bias, does not have an easily identifiable measurement or social indicator component, and is not usually integrated with the existing community policy structure.

Delphi or Group Diagnosis Method

The Delphi process and modifications of it are currently very popular in community problem solving. The basic technique developed by the Rand Corporation is a *process* survey method for predicting alternative futures. Individual surveys or interviews are conducted of a relatively small but well-selected group. The data are used to shape consensus toward common goals and policies. There is a substantial body of literature on this method and its many variations (Johnston & Wilson, 1974).

The basic liability of this method is that it is "expert" centered. That is, the persons providing the information—

the input—to this system are preselected. In some cases such persons may not reflect total local concerns and interest.

Macrostructural Methods

Frank Young and Ruth Young (1968) have popularized a method of researching communities using unobtrusive measures. The Youngs and others propose that an examination of physical and social institutions, or "institution tracking" as MacCannell (1974) labels it, in a given community predicts social dimensions (i.e. political cohesion), which were discussed previously. The methodology involved requires collecting large quantities of secondary data on relevant social, political, and commercial enterprise and scaling (usually Guttman scales) for comparative analyses. Eberts and Sigmondo (1974) have refined this method for policy use by incorporating time series data to analyze civic or community growth and change patterns.

Although this method is extremely useful in larger-scale analyses (e.g., countries, states, and counties), it is deficient as a policy tool for local neighborhoods and city governments, and it does not provide for local citizen involvement in the analytical process.

Opinion or Attitude Surveys

Sampling public opinion by questionnaire or interview is a widely used and accepted technique to ascertain community needs. This method is usually and best employed when the specific data are required related to a particular program or service. It is easier to measure the degree of satisfaction or dissatisfaction in a survey than to determine individual or group needs. Surveys are enormously useful and feasible for community development diagnoses, as demonstrated by Christensen's work in North Carolina

(1974) and Dilman and Dobash's related work in Washington (1972), where massive amounts of information in citizen attitudes and desires were identified.

Translating surveys into policy is a delicate process, and monitoring the impacts of the policy using survey exclusively may not be entirely feasible for economic reasons.

The approaches discussed above offer only a brief analysis of the major current community diagnostic and policy processes. Each of these methods has assets and liabilities. The major limitation of these approaches for the current city context is that most of them (1) have limited capacity for linkage with the existing governmental and related policy process; (2) do not offer a means to develop social indicators, benchmarks, or monitoring systems; (3) require the assembly of data difficult to interpret by local decision makers; or (4) lack direct citizen involvement.

It is our view that the community development *process* for cities must be firmly anchored in a theoretical paradigm that provides policy guidance and yields accountability standard with the city as both a geographic and policy entity. Such a paradigm can be forged out of each of the existing community development models previously described with some effort. However, we believe that the existing methodologies, as combined in the social marketing model, meet many of the above requirements and build on as well as integrate earlier efforts into a coherent useful strategy. The need for a multilevel policy paradigm for rural and regional development is recognized by Eberts and Sigmondo (1974), but a similar framework has not emerged using the city as the principle focus.

THE CONCEPT AND MODEL

Americans are not at ease with the notion of marketing public goods and services to our communities, cities, and states. Only recently have state and local economic development commissions been able to use tax dollars to advertise the virtues of certain locations to attract business to areas in order to expand local job opportunities and improve local tax bases. The idea of state and local tax-supported industrial development is still struggling to gain acceptance, but it is becoming apparent that the city itself and its related taxing authorities (school districts, etc.) must become more conscious of their own marketing capacities and responsibilities (Drucker, 1958). However, we have grown accustomed to politicians packaging themselves, their campaigns, and their political promises. In fact, Maginnes, in the *Selling of the President* (1969) and White, in the *Making of a President* (1972), suggest that we anticipate politicians to be good products marketed well!

The advent of inner-city blight and urban flight indicates further that the city, both large urban and small rural, must become involved in a widened marketing strategy if it is to survive. As Kotler (n.d.) so aptly notes:

> The process of city administration is invisible to the citizen who sees little evidence of its human components but feels the sharp pain of taxation. With increasingly poor public services, his desires are more insistently expressed. Yet his expression needs seem to issue into thin air for government does not appear to be attentive to his needs. (p. 3)

Very little research has examined cities as marketing entities, to address the issues cited by Kotler. Shapiro (1975) discusses nonprofit organizations, which resemble cities in some respects. The city has several unique functions in that it provides service (fire, sewer, health, etc.) while it has regulatory and control responsibilities (zoning, licensing, taxing, and police). Shapiro, however, relegates marketing in government organizations to politics and political science. Although much can be said in support of his argument that most activity within the city has political characteristics, there are many components that are directly or indirectly related to the marketing model. In spite of his reservations, Shapiro suggests that there is some potential for applying marketing thinking to most nonprofit situations, including government. Sparks (n.d.) specifically discussed the role of marketing in public bureaucracies. He concludes that there is a major role that marketing principles can play in operating a more efficient and meaningful public bureaucracy, but he does not offer a strategy to effect this system.

It appears to us that although private nonprofit organizations may in some ways be a simpler arena for application of marketing principles, in fact, the utilization of these principles within the community is both valid and necessary. It is our view that changes that have taken place both internal and external to the city have made it mandatory for the growth and stability of the city to utilize some of the thinking and methodology that is currently applied in the commercial marketing sector to the delivery of public goods and services. Kotler's broad definition of marketing is that it is a "set of human activities directed at facilitating and consumating exchanges." (Kotler, 1973). Our definition of public marketing is a modification of the American Marketing Association's language that discusses marketing as "the performance of (public) activities that direct the flow of goods and services from producer to consumer or user" (AMA, 1960).

Let us examine some of the factors that we believe contribute to the appropriate application of marketing principles to communities. The first is the advent of a national New Federalism policy, which transfers much of the responsibility for community development from the federal level to the state, county, and individual communities. Local governments are using revenue sharing funds from the new Housing and Community Development Act (H/CD) to begin to restructure their institutions for economic, social, and physical planning. The greatest current need that cities face is to determine the appropriate allocation of their resources based on locally assessed needs and priorities instead of merely engaging in police activities (issuing permits, maintaining streets, etc.). Another related factor is the increased sophistication of the community resident that has taken place through the media, consumer organizations, and greater involvement of the individual resident in community affairs at every level. Attendant to this latter factor is the increased concern, in fact, militancy, of certain segments of the community in influencing the allocation of community resources. Groups such as the aged, economic and ethnic minorities, youth groups, and so on are now much more highly organized and vocal, and they vie effectively for attention and funds from the city treasury. The majority of communities utilize a city manager system that tends to be relatively independent of politics. This may allow for a more independent, rational, and continuous set of programs. Last, citizens increasingly have found the polling place, with its attendant political campaigns, more and more a popularity contest and less and less satisfying as a way of communicating their needs and concerns about their community. Recently, the energy crisis and concerns for ecological consideration increased the complexity involved in satisfying the community's needs.

All of the above factors have served as an impetus for comprehensive planning for community economic and social development by cities themselves instead of waiting for counties or states to do it for them. Typically, community development efforts that have been mounted have been ones that use more traditional or short-term methods to deal with a narrow range of physical development or economic problems. Our view is that if one considers the city as a source of goods and services and both the residents and the business/industry sectors as consumers of these goods and services, much practical value can be gained from analyzing the community within a marketing model, and meaningful changes can be made to produce efficient community development by utilizing marketing methods.

Before we look at the specific applications of marketing techniques to community development activities, let us examine the general character of the community in relation to the business and private nonprofit organization. (See Figure 6–1). Business firms, once operational, receive their funds from the sale of goods and services to customers, whereas in private nonprofit organizations, funds for operation are primarily received from donors instead of from some type of customer. The city represents a much more complex model in that funds for operation come directly from the consumers in the form of property taxes, sales tax, special bond assessments, and so on. However, the community also receives redistributed funds from the country and state level as well as federal funds which, although derived ultimately from tax revenue, are not under the direct control of the resident consumer. In some instances state and federal funds must be obtained on a competitive basis. This complexity presents a challenge in terms of understanding the community within the marketing framework; we believe it also presents an opportunity to clarify the various roles played by the consumer resident and other sources of funding so as to be able to produce a more rational community growth and development plan. The customer in the commercial marketplace has a variety of choices to select from as far as the types of goods and services that are available and the particular brands and sizes within brands. The commercial consumer also is usually quite mobile and can select from local sources, may travel to communities other than his or her own and, by using the mail, can purchase goods from throughout the world. On the other hand, within the community the consumer is more a captive; homes, schools, parks, recreation facilities, health facilities, and police and fire protection are

Figure 6-1 (a) Marketing models: private, nonprofit. (b) Marketing models: city. (Adapted from Shapiro, 1975.)

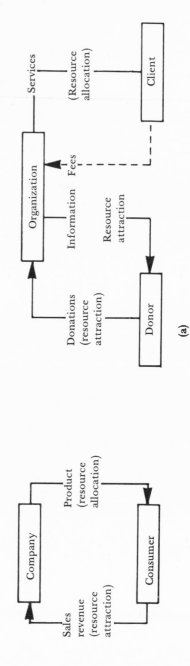

(a)

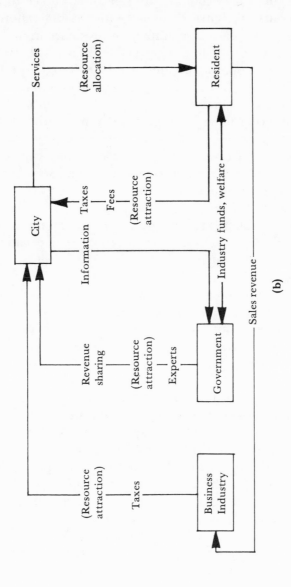

(b)

such that they ordinarily do not allow choice to operate. Obviously, the citizen can make the determination that for a variety of reasons, maintaining residence in that particular community is no longer viable, as many thousands are learning in our major cities. To the extent that children, as they leave high school, move away and do not return to the community or that adult residents move to other communities in order to satisfy their needs, the sources of revenue supplied by these individuals is lost to the city. On a more fundamental level, the city or community can be said to have *failed* in the provision of goods and services that satisfy their consumer residents, particularly when consumers are, in fact, a heterogenous population. In the past the failure to satisfy the resident in a meaningful way has been viewed, except for rare exceptions in some urban areas, as a minor consequence. Today, as pointed out earlier, these are becoming of major consequence. The events leading up to the problems of major cities such as New York, San Francisco, and Boston point out vividly what can happen if a relatively captive resident is continually led down the path of dissatisfaction. As blacks, Chicanos, women, and others aspire to achieve equal benefits from the political system, this unleashes active, often hostile, forces within the social fabric. In essence, the city is no longer made up of superficially homogeneous groups ("ghettoized") but of heterogenous components whose interests become the focal point of the total city political process.

Just as the marketing task for profit-making organizations includes the basic marketing function of facilitating and consumating exchanges, the community as a marketing organization has a similar responsibility. This includes viewing consumers not as one homogenous group, but as made up of various segments. The city must then know its segments and their needs and demands. Another factor, however, that operates in the community is not only that it must market goods to the consumer and industry/business sectors, but must also market the community to the state and federal organizations so as to increase the likelihood of receiving funds that will help the community to achieve its broader mission. Communities no longer can meet the demands of their residents only with locally produced resources. It is mandatory, then, that the various state and federal resources be tapped in order to provide high-cost items such as capital improvements. Naturally, these resources are also limited and thus the community must present its needs to the funding agencies in a way that enhances as highly as possible the likelihood of receiving funds in a competitive marketplace.

Another difference between private concerns and cities is that a company is judged in terms of the profit that it makes for its stockholders, whereas in the community the criteria for success should be the satisfaction of the consumer. It would be fair to say that many or most of the residents in a community are not aware of the complex relationships between the goods and services that the city offers and the sources of revenue available to fund those goods and services. It is much more likely that they respond to very personal feelings about community management or service management, as represented by members of the city council and school superintendents. Since the citizen is both a consumer and manager or stockholder, he or she has the right and desire to voice opinions on the ultimate product and on the mode of delivery. Let us consider the complex marketing model of the city as illustrated in Figure 6–2.

Public Marketing Components

Shapiro (1975) points out that the basic marketing task can be divided into three major components: resource attraction, resource allocation, and persuasion. The resource at-

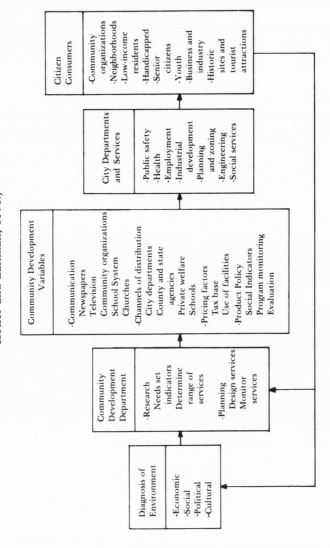

Figure 6-2 Public marketing for community development: a systems approach. (Adapted from Kotler and Zaltman, 1971.)

traction activity in profit-making firms is a financial one in which funds may be attracted from banking sources but are primarily monies generated by the sale of goods and services. The resource allocation function in the profit-making firm involves all the decisions that result in various advertising, capital, research development, and related decisions. In the city resource attraction sources, as pointed out earlier, come from both the funds received from consumer residents and businesses through taxes and the attraction of funds from state, county, and federal agencies. Resource allocation in the community would involve all the decisions concerned with the various goods and services that are potentially offered by a community. In contrast, in a profit-making organization there is a direct feedback mechanism from the consumer with regard to resource allocation and resource attraction. However, the basic marketing concept, which stresses the importance of satisfying consumer needs, would certainly seem to apply in both instances.

The use of the market model in public decision making is well grounded in the theory of interaction and exchange, as suggested by Presthus (1974).

> Interaction theory rests essentially upon two well established principles from psychology and economics. The psychological principle is that all behavior is determined by differential reinforcement. . . . Economic theory contributes the assumption that individuals bring to personal relationships a more-or-less rational calculus which ensures that a given interaction will be continued only if the sum total of benefits received equals or preferably outweighs the costs of time, energy and commitment expended in all such activities. A cost-benefit equilibrium is sought.

Weber's work (1966) further amplifies this conceptual framework and places it in the context of the city when he says:

> We wish to speak of a "city" only in cases where the local inhabitants satisfy an economically substantial part of their daily wants in the local market.

The Weber market assumes a supply of public goods and services as well as private exchanges.

In the following sections, we explore the Presthus/ Weber paradigm as it relates to community development methods.

Resource Attraction

The community must attract its resources in several ways. People themselves represent a resource in that the occupation of a residence within the community ordinarily automatically results in certain benefits available to the community. These include the ones mentioned earlier in the chapter, such as property tax and other levies that occur when the consumer chooses to be a resident in a particular community. In addition, sources are attracted from county, state, and federal agencies through mechanisms such as a standard formula based on population size, need, and occasionally through application involving competitive proposals for particular community development projects.

The attraction of these resources in a community utilizes the standard marketing techniques or persuasion, which will be discussed in more detail later. However, it is obvious that successful persuasion of the consumers to vote themselves increased taxes has not met with spectacular success. It is, and has been, very difficult to pin down the exact source of failure in the attraction of resources for the community and, in fact, it has been easy for each component of the community to place the blame in such a complex situation on every other function or individual in a community instead of on itself.

Another critical area for resource attraction is retail businesses and industrial activities. These sectors help through tax revenues and jobs to establish a more subjective sense of accomplishment or pride in the community; this might occur when a community adds a favorable image

retail establishment or perhaps avoids one that has negative connotations.

Resource Allocation

The first basic decision in resource allocation is to determine what is the function of the particular community. In
other words, what are the objectives for that community?
After this decision is made, one can determine which goods
and services should be allocated to the community and at
what level. The decision must be made as to whether these
goods or services should be available to all neighborhoods
to the same degree, or if individual segments of the population should receive special goods and services, such as
youth, the aged, the economically deprived, and ethnic
groups. For the city, this is obviously a very complex task,
since the city provides a wide variety of goods and services
that involve different types of individuals, equipment, and
facilities in order to deliver such goods and services effectively. As Sandage and Fryburger (1966) point out, in our
economy these decisions are usually reached based on psychological factors instead of on an assessment of physiolog-
ical need. Therefore, psychological assessment and
motivation play a key role in the distribution of goods and
the response to citizen requests for services.

Persuasion

Persuasion is a third marketing function for the community; it includes two major components. The first is persuading extramural sources such as state and federal
organizations to supply funds and/or expert help in order
to accomplish community objectives. The second type of
persuasion function is the one involved in persuading the
consumer residents to take some action with regard to the

community. Lazersfeld and Merton (1958), in one of their earliest papers on social organization, describe this process in a manner that remains true nearly three decades later. Things such as volunteer activity for the health, school and other sectors, participation in the voting process, attraction of people from outlying areas to the city proper, and persuading people to maintain residence in the community are examples of such a persuasion function (Lazersfeld & Merton, 1960). It is interesting to note that almost the only effort that cities and communities make to persuade individuals to come to a particular area involves the attraction for business of tourists during the area's tourist season. It is remarkable how little is done to communicate the values for more permanent residency in a community. Perhaps the only exception to this has been the efforts in California, Florida, and Arizona, in which new communities have been constructed and efforts have been made to persuade individuals to settle there permanently. These efforts have involved a variety of marketing techniques.

Other areas in which the persuasion function operates for a community are in convincing people to change their attitudes and practices in the use of limited resources such as energy, anti-litter campaigns, utilization of community facilities such as parks and swimming pools, and the contribution to other voluntary activities within the community.

Much persuasion effort, whether successful or not, has been directed toward increasing the utilization of downtown core areas by residents. Perhaps the lack of success of these programs is partly because appropriate marketing techniques have not been utilized or only partially used.

Social Marketing Tools that Can Be Used for Community Development

Kotler and Zaltman (1973) suggested that marketing strategies could be utilized to promote social change. They limited their analyses and discussion to the traditional non-profit social agency, but their model certainly has fairly wide application to city community development activities. Borrowing from the Kotler-Zaltman model and from the early work of Shapiro and others, the following techniques appear to be applicable in the current context.

COMMUNICATIONS.   The members of a community have various communication techniques available for use in carrying out its marketing functions. Most communities have one or more newspapers that can be utilized by the city management as a method of delivering information to their citizens. In some areas a local radio station or cable television can be used to present meetings and other special activities to the city council. In addition, annual reports and other special brochures can be developed and distributed to all the members of the community. The various city departments can themselves have techniques for communicating their functions, such as the practice of having police and fire personnel give information lectures in the schools and the more recent technique of having students accompany police officers on their daily rounds. Also, some communities encourage students to play various roles within the community management structure in order to understand the operation of a city better.

It would appear mandatory that if resource attraction from residents is to occur, the managers of the city must communicate what they want to do, the alternatives, and how they expect the residents' contribution to occur; they must do this in a meaningful way in order to expect any degree of cooperation.

Obviously, communication plays a critical role in the persuasion function; however, the community also may use communications in resource attraction and allocation. In the areas of attraction, certainly communications concerning how funds are utilized and their source can be useful in attracting revenue from the resident. Also, communication through specialized brochures and proposals to state and federal organizations can be critical in the attraction of funds to the community. In resource allocation more efficient utilization of the allocated resources can take place if the residents are fully aware of the variety of facilities and activities that the community has to offer.

CHANNELS OF DISTRIBUTION.   For the profit-making organization, channels of distribution include the standard wholesale distributor, the banker, and the retail organization. However, for the community, channels of distribution range from ones that go directly into individual households (e.g., water, electricity, and gas), to ones where the consumer goes to other locations (e.g., parks, hospitals, and schools). Some services are distributed primarily on the basis of unique events, such as fires and police activities and others, such as welfare, require the individual to report to certain offices at certain times. Many of these activities have location as a common characteristic. Thus, the degree of satisfaction that a consumer can receive will depend to a great extent on the availability of the goods and services. This may include, in addition to physical location, days and/or times of the day at which the particular goods or service is made available. Certainly, basic decisions with regard to the location of shopping centers, whether in a core downtown section or in suburban locations, will have direct effects on the satisfactions of the residents of a community. Utilization of various school and health services will depend to a great extent on the propinquity and ease of use of such services. In some cases, language and/or cultural barriers may act as a deterrent to the utilization of some goods and services.

The recent rulings on busing to insure equality of educational opportunity are certainly a distribution activity that may be mandated by the courts.

PRICING.   Pricing as a marketing tool is directly related to the ability to attract resources. Obviously, the more that a private firm can maintain sales volume and increase prices, the more profit it will make. However, in the community, pricing is a more complex activity. Some things naturally are a direct matter of exchange of money for services, such as the price for use of a municipal pool, tennis courts, and so on. For other areas, pricing is a function that may be outside the realm of the community, such as the price for energy resources, gasoline, electricity, and natural gas. The indirect pricing activities where price in a sense represents the tax assessment for particular activities such as schools is not as amenable to a simple analysis. However, there should be a relationship between the price (i.e., the amount of taxes that are paid) and the quality of the product that is received by the resident. When this does not occur and there is a discrepancy or apparent discrepancy between quality and service and the perceived price that the consumer pays, the dissatisfaction that results can lead to many unpleasant consequences. For example, the next levy vote, although absolutely essential for maintainance of an activity, may not be approved. In many cases, since consumer residents are not charged directly for the use of certain goods and services, it is very difficult to make the connection between the types and levels of goods and services available and what monies are required to support such activities. Clearly, the role of communication is one that would be essential in order to improve on this lack of understanding. When price changes are required, it would appear to be essential that information concerning the alternatives and reasons underlying the change of price be communicated in an effective fashion to the consumer resident.

In another area, the community prices its proposals for the funds and services that it desires from extramural sources. No doubt the relationships between what the community proposes to do and the level of funding and type of expert services it thinks are necessary to accomplish it could be a significant factor in the atttraction of extramural resources to the community.

It may seem apparent, but the price that one charges for the use of tennis courts, swimming pools, and so on and the level of utilization by the consumer resident is really not very different from what occurs when a consumer makes a choice among various canned soup products in the supermarket. However, in the community situation, not only will the consumer perhaps go outside the community to have these needs satisfied but, in addition, the dissatisfaction with the community will have its effect on the future willingness of that resident to support a voluntary activity or vote for increased taxes. Another more subjective price that is paid by residents is what they have to give up in order to maintain residency in a particular community. Consumer residents pay a price in that living in a particular community may make it inconvenient for them to enjoy a symphony, opera, sports, or other activities that are not available to them in the community. Also, the price may be in terms of the time and effort they volunteer for community activities. What is returned in value for this price is the other goods and services that are offered by the community to the individual. The question is whether or not these are of sufficient magnitude to justify being a resident and making a contribution to a particular community. For some people the price of living in a particular community is the admission to others that, in fact, they are residents of that community. Some areas have such strong negative connotations that the residents do not admit to association with a particular community or, at the first opportunity, they leave.

PRODUCT POLICY.   Product policy basically is the determination of which goods and services are made available to the consumer. In the community, the definition of product and services is unquestionably the most critical aspect of the marketing process. The wide diversity of goods and services and the variety of segments in the population for which various goods and services are appropriate make product policy aspects of the community one of the most important and difficult areas. In addition to offering a product or service to the resident, the community also has, in a sense, a policy with regard to what types of extramural funding and expertise it decides that it needs and attempts to acquire.

There are many product policy decisions that are critical for the community. Should the community attempt to offer services or goods that will be attractive to the unemployed, to ethnic minorities, or to the senior citizen? To do so obviously means the attraction of these individuals to the community. What are the trade-offs among various services that the community might offer, and how would revenue sources be made available to support such activities? If the assortment and type and quality of products and services that are available to the community are not satisfactory, then one can be certain that eventually the resource attraction process will be severely hampered either from the loss of residents themselves to other communities or from the unwillingness of the community to assess itself for the cost of such services or to volunteer its own time and effort on their behalf.

MARKETING RESEARCH.   An area in which communities have been the least sensitive and active is marketing research. What work that has been accomplished has been in determining the community resources by using techniques such as a community profile or social indicators that essentially catalog the available resources in a community. No one, including us, can deny the importance of this information which, unfortunately, in many cases is not communicated effectively to the consumer resident. However, there is another very important area of social marketing research that has been relatively untapped. This area is the one of determining the consumer resident attitudes, practices, and knowledge with regard to the community. It is here that the core of the marketing concept lies. If one is to satisfy the consumer as a basic objective, then one must know what the consumer feels, thinks, and does with regard to community offerings, both present and future. Certainly, the techniques utilized by private firms in determining such information from various segments of the consuming population are available for use by investigators in the community development area. From such research, community development investigators can get a picture of how the present goods and services are used or, in many cases, are not used. The degree of satisfaction with these goods and services and some idea of what types of goods and services would be desired by the population can also be determined. In addition, by analyzing the results for various geographical, ethnic, income, or other relevant segments of the population, some of the differences and similarities among these groups can be ascertained; thus product policy decision makers can have a much better grasp of the trade-offs that might be involved in satisfying particular needs for products and services.

Utilizing marketing research techniques is an important initial activity in the marketing of a community. Such techniques can be used by the city or community to determine attitudes toward proposed changes in the goods or services that have recently been initiated. It may be appropriate in some cases to build in a standard feedback mechanism for individual areas of the city, such as police, park, and recreation.

One of the values of the research of this type is to provide guidelines in the resource allocation process; in addition, research results can be fed back through communications to the consumer residents along with appropriate educational material. Thus, through the use of persuasion techniques, different attitudes and/or utilization of goods and services may result.

Resource attraction in the area of retail and industrial establishments could benefit considerably from the results of marketing research activities. It is very likely that many of the dissatisfactions, goals, and desires of retail and industrial sectors of the community may be in opposition to those of the resident and thus require careful analysis of a community's total objectives in order to develop an appropriate trade-off model.

Marketing research, in addition to determining what various segments in a community have in common as well as do not share, can serve another very important end; through careful analysis of marketing research data, segments can be identified and characterized that may not have been visible before the study was conducted. What on the surface might appear to be a reasonable segmentation in terms of geographical location might turn out to be a segmentation based on income or ethnic background. It is clear that unless the homogeneous segments in the community are appropriately identified, resource allocation can only be partially successful.

CONCLUSIONS

The previous discussion illustrates that the marketing model can supply insights into the operation of the community. More important, it can provide tools by which the community can more efficiently determine and implement the goals for its constituents.

The application of this frame of reference is even more critical for the community than it is for the private organization, since the private organization has feedback mechanisms that have much shorter time lags and are much more direct. If the private company is not meeting the needs of its customers, it will shortly fail as a profit maker. However, unfortunately for the community, the time lag is much longer and the feedback much less direct; thus, inappropriate decisions are made both by those who are managers and administrators within the community and by the consumer residents and business sectors of the community. It is imperative that the various components of the community have a means of more clearly defining the objectives, trade-offs, and resources of a community, and that they can do this as quickly as is feasible. The result of not accomplishing these objectives, although it may not occur as quickly as it does in the private sector, just as certainly does occur; when it does, the retrieval activities must be heroic. In the aftermath of such a failure the spirit of a community can be essentially lost. Unfortunately, there are sufficient examples of cities that have arrived at this state.

We believe it is entirely within the realm of possibility to analyze a community utilizing the framework presented here and the methodologies proposed to provide an effective, vital and successful community development programs. Furthermore, the paradigm we suggest offers a means to integrate the disparate and sometimes confusing methods and techniques of community development into a system that relates to the realities of modern city government.

In the next chapter I (Blakely) advance and illustrate a more direct and simple systems approach within the same framework. The choice of methods clearly depends on the practitioner's orientation, time, and resources.

An Illustration of Public Marketing in a Community Development Program

In Yuba City, California (population 30,000 with suburbs), a public marketing approach is being experimented with through the participation and assistance of local colleges and universities. The citizens of Yuba City (the buyer or purchaser market) will be offered the opportunity to provide the local governing body (the city council) with their preferences through use of a citywide questionnaire. The community executive structure (city manager and department heads) will attempt to process this information, tabulate the cost-benefits analyses, and disseminate this data back to the residents in a handbook. Town meetings will then be organized throughout the city and suburbs to develop a clear set of goals and priorities from the citizens themselves. After these community meetings are held and preferences for resource allocations selected, the local government will be responsible for representing these desires in the form of a "Civic Action Plan."

The Yuba City Goals program is a unique blend of elitist, pluralist community organization and market models for decision making. It utilizes many of the traditional approaches to community development, but recasts them in a total systems orientation that is easily comprehensible by both the layperson and the public official. The city governing structure in this model takes on the role of a marketing organization by articulating community desires into policy outputs. The representative capacity of local government will be tested by this experiment by the pluralist activities generated through the questionnaire, sampling, and town meeting techniques.

The Yuba City experiment provides an opportunity to examine whether community development models, which are highly dependent on face-to-face and group interaction, have the vitality for modern governmental decision making. The public marketing model was suggested by the city council and administration as the clearest and most relevant means of developing a framework for community input in the highly sociotechnical and political process of modern city government.

BIBLIOGRAPHY AND REFERENCES

Alchin, E. W. *A reconnaisance research plan for community development.* A Technical Bulletin, B-49. The Institute for Community Development and Services, Michigan State.

American Marketing Association, *Marketing definitions: A glossary of marketing terms.* Chicago: American Marketing Association, 1960.

Batten, T. R. *Communities and their development.* London: Oxford University Press, 1957.

Biddle, W., & Biddle, Louride. *The community development process.* New York: Holt, Rinehart and Winston, Inc., 1965.

Blakely, E. J. *The new federalism: Implications for community development in non-metropolitan areas.* Davis, Calif.: University of California Community Development Research Service, July 1975.

Cary, L. *Community development as a process.* Columbia, Mo.: University of Missouri Press, 1970.

Christensen, J. *Through our eyes.* Vols. 1, 2, and 4. Raleigh, N.C.: Agricultural Extension Service, North Carolina State University, 1974.

Clewett, R. L., & Olson, J. *Social indicators and marketing.* New York: American Marketing Association, 1974.

Dilman, D. A., & Dobash, R. *Preferences for community living and their implications for population redistribution.* Pullman, Wash.: Washington State Agricultural Experiment Station, November 1972.

Drucker, P. F. Marketing & Economic Development. *Journal of Marketing.* 1958, **5**, (3), 252–259.

Elberts, P. R. A Multi-Level Policy Research Paradigm: Implications for Rural and Regional Development. A paper presented at the Annual Meetings of the Rural Sociological Society, San Francisco, 1975.

Eberts, P. R., & Sandau, J. Differentiation in Macro Structures: Its Nature and Continuity Through Time. A paper presented at the Annual Meeting of the Rural Sociological Society, San Francisco, 1975.

Eberts, P. R., & Sigmondo, S. A Multi-Level Policy Research Paradigm for Rural and Regional Development. A paper presented at the Annual Meeting of the Rural Sociological Society, August 1974.

Greenberg, S. *The quality of mercy.* New York: Atheneum, 1971.

Johnston, A. P., & Wilson, M. From private to public sector planning: Missing values and the need for adaptation. *Educational Planning,* 1974, **1** (2).

Kotler, M. *Community forum.* Unpublished and undated.

———. A marketing orientation for government agencies. Unpublished paper. Evanston, Ill.: Northwestern University, February 1972.

Kotler, M. A generic concept of marketing. *Journal of Marketing,* 1973, **35** (3), 46–54.

Kotler, M., & Zaltman, G. Social Marketing: An Approach to Planned Social Change. *Journal of Marketing,* 1973, **35** 3–12.

Lazersfeld, P. F., & Merton, R. Mass communication, popular task and organized social action. Wilbur Schromm, (Ed.), *Moss Communication,* Urbana, Ill.: University of Illinois Press, 1960.

MacCannell, D. & Young, R. Predicting quality of life in the united states. A paper presented at the Annual Meeting of the Rural Sociological Society, San Francisco, 1974.

Maginnes, J. *The selling of the president.* New York: Trident Press, 1969.

Martin, N. A. The outlandish idea: How a marketing man would save India. *Marketing/Communication,* 1968, **96** (3).

Nix, H., et al., *Community social action series.* Vol. 1–6. Athens, Ga.: Institute of Community and Area Development, University of Georgia, 1965.

Poston, R. *Democracy speaks many tongues.* New York: Harper & Row, 1962.

Presthus, R. *Elites in the policy process.* London: Cambridge University Press, 1974.

Rosove, P. A trend impact matrix for societal impact assessment. *Educational Planning,* 1974, **1** (2), 67–79.

Sandage, C. H., & Fryburger, V. *The role of advertising: A book of readings.* Homewood, Ill.: Richard D. Irwin, 1960. pp. 257–65.

Sargeant, C. Decision making systems and planned change. *Journal of the Community Development Society,* Spring 1973, **4** (1), 115.

Schneider, L. M. *Marketing urban mass transit.* Boston: Harvard University, 1965.

Shapiro, B. Marketing in non-profit organizations. *Journal of Voluntary Action Research,* 1975, **3** (3–4),

Simon, J. L. A huge marketing research task—Birth Control. *Journal of Marketing Research,* 1968, **5** (1), 21–27.

Social progress through community development. United Nations Publications, 1959.

Sparks, M. Public marketing: The development of a systematic perspective in public bureaucracies. Unpublished paper, School of Public Administration, University of Southern California, no date.

Warren, R. *Studying your community.* (2nd ed.) New York: The Free Press, 1968.

Webb, K. & Hatry, H. *Obtaining citizen feedback: The application of citizen surveys to local government.* Washington, D.C.: The Urban Institute, 1973.

Weber, M. The nature of the city. In *Warren Perspectives on the American Community.* New York: Rand McNally, 1966.

White, T. *The making of the president.* A series 1960, 1964, 1968, and 1972, New York, Harper & Row.

Young, F. A structural approach to development. *Journal of Developing Areas,* 1968, **2,** 363–376.

Zatlman, G., & Vertinsky, I. Health marketing: A suggested model. *Journal of Marketing,* July 1971, 19–27.

Chapter 7

THE COMMUNITY DIAGNOSTIC METHOD: AN APPROACH TO THE APPLICATION OF COMMUNITY DEVELOPMENT RESEARCH

Edward J. Blakely

BACKGROUND

The effective organization of citizens in communities and the gaining of their participation in problem solving has always been a significant dilemma. Modern social planners have developed sophisticated methods to ascertain the economic, political, and social ills of a community. The knowledge of these scientists combined with existing technology should resolve nearly all community problems. Fortunately or unfortunately, human beings have not designed their life systems based on empirical research evidence; they are based on more fundamental and frequently less rational grounds. Social scientists are not able to translate their ideas easily or quickly into public policy because few social organizations (communities, groups, etc.) comprehend the desirability of *change*.

*Another version of this chapter was published in the *International Technical Cooperation Center Review,* July 19, 1976, **13.**

Therefore, in order to analyze a community's problems, needs, and aspirations effectively, the social scientist must be prepared to examine the norms, or mores of the group he or she is studying (Sanders, 1960). The methods and tools that social scientists employ for gaining this data vary, depending on their specialization. For example, psychologists and sociologists might use questionnaires or interviews to determine the nature and extent of a problem; anthropologists, given the same community, might utilize a number of different observation techniques to describe the issue. Community developers, unlike other social scientists, identify the nature and scope of the problem and are also responsible for developing and implementing a solution(s). In scientific lexicon this means that the community developer is involved in theory generating, hypothesis stating, or *descriptive analysis* and in finding a remedy or prescriptive analysis (Blakely, 1972). This places a heavy burden on the development specialist, since he or she is held accountable for the initial diagnosis, the program implementation, the community response, and the ultimate result. The community developer's tasks are even greater, since the tools for accurately determining or diagnosing the nature, scope, intensity, and shape of the problem are only imprecisely developed in community development.

DEFINING AND DESCRIBING THE DIAGNOSTIC SUBSYSTEM

The misidentification of community problems is the bane of all development efforts. We can all cite "horror stories" in development where inappropriate or inaccurate diagnosis led to results damaging to the client system or the practitioner(s) involved.

Communities require many things. Community needs can seldom be reduced to information, skills, or knowledge. It is unlikely, for instance, that a community without adequate natural resources (water, power, etc.) will prosper, regardless of the enlightenment of its citizens. Therefore, the assessment process in any community must involve a thorough analyis of the total community's economic, social, cultural, environmental, and other problems before intervention strategies can be designed. Community development techniques contribute significant methodology to the diagnostic process, but most of their approaches are not sufficient (McMahon, 1970). In this chapter I merge these techniques into a comprehensive system that integrates the principal features of each and provides an organized useful means for practitioners to apply research data in field situations.

DEFINITIONS

The terms "needs assessment" and "community analysis" are used interchangeably in community development. Although both terms refer to diagnostic processes, they are not the same. "Needs assessment" is a phrase referring to individual perceptions and desires. Community analysis usually describes the social, economic, and environmental diagnoses used in the community development process to determine structure and individual and group capacities.

There is a tendency for community developers to apply a single favorite diagnostic approach to all community problems without differentiation. This is analogous to a physician using *one* diagnostic procedure regardless of the patient's symptoms. Clearly, communities and community problems bear a great deal of similarity throughout the world. But it is also apparent that while there may be fairly uniform patterns, the particular problem, issue, or difficulty manifests itself uniquely within a specific town, area, state, or region. Consequently, the diagnostic process must be adaptable to the type of problem situation encountered as well as to the specific process utilized according to either the intended outcome (yield) or the particular aspect of the problem studied (Farmer, Sheats, & Deshler 1972). For example, the diagnostic technique used in identifying the target population for a family planning program may not be applicable in determining the means to implement the same program. Diagnosis, then, is the technique and process of ascertaining the nature, scope, and intensity of community problems and of identifying the intervention strategies applicable in the situation.

The comprehensive community development diagnostic model incorporates the principal analytical features of community and organizational development. The comprehensive diagnostic model consists of five phases: (1) prediagnosis—an entry or familiarization step; (2) diagnostic entry—formal data collection; (3) tentative intervention design—experimental intervention models; (4) trial interventions—testing various strategies; and (5) diagnostic evaluation—assembling diagnostic feedback for program design (CRUSK, 1972). Each phase requires a more detailed explanation. The phases are also summarized in Table 7–1.

PREDIAGNOSTIC

This is the most important step in the diagnostic process. The practitioner must first "size up" the community in which he or she will operate. This process must be engaged in without any preplanned data-gathering design that might hamper significant insights or overlook potential areas for future inquiry. During this period the practitioner should identify the general size, shape, and physical barriers in the area. This process includes creating a social map of the community that indicates where various socioeco-

Table 7-1 The Comprehensive Community Development Diagnostic Model

Phase	Purpose	Method(s)	Yield
1. Prediagnostic	Familiarization with initial impressions of problems	Visual surveys and unstructured interviews; participant observation	Information on the physical and social boundaries of the client system
2. Diagnostic entry	Formal data gathering	Census studies and demographic studies; surveys, observations	Needs and problems of target population—community socioeconomic and leadership structure
3. Tentative intervention design	Developing various intervention models	Experimental models force field analysis of various approaches	Selection of intervention strategies
4. Trial interventions	Testing intervention strategies	Simulations; experimental and control groups	Design of intervention methods
5. Diagnostic evaluation	Data assembling on all	Comparative analysis; expert consultation; participant consultation	Analysis of project or program potential in relationship to the community's needs the problem, and the impact on the socioeconomic structure

nomic groups live, work, and play. Physical features such as hills, streets, expressways, streams, or rivers that might hamper intergroup relations should be carefully noted. An overlay map of the location of civic clubs, community associations, churches, and other organizational structures should be compared with housing, race, and other demographic data. In addition, the practitioner must "walk the areas" to experience the way(s) in which people live, talk, and act toward one another and "outsiders." This preanalysis or intuitive look at the community will provide important information on how the community must be approached for any in-depth data gathering. Certain types of surveys, questionnaires, or other means of acquiring information will be eliminated, while others will suggest themselves. These "first impression" data should be carefully recorded for comparison with future information during the diagnostic process and subsequent program evaluation.

The purpose of maintaining "first impression" or prediagnostic data is that they provide a baseline for later program evaluation. Although the data collected in program design may be objective, the practitioners bring their subjectivity to the analysis.

Among the best sources for a more extensive discussion of the prediagnostic process are works in the new field of organizational development (OD). Many of the published research studies in OD provide relevant insights into diagnostic systems, with a strong emphasis on prediagnostic methodologies, (Bowers, & Seashore, 1970; Rice, 1958). In their text on planned change, Lippitt, Watson, and Westley (1958) offer some of the theoretical background for how the entire orientation to diagnosis is the key step in organizational change. Of course, with some interpretation, one can see how the OD diagnostic process can be an important tool in the community change process.

DIAGNOSTIC ENTRY

This is the formal data-gathering activity on the client system. The prediagnosis should provide the practitioner with a fairly well-defined notion of the boundaries of the client system, its beliefs or values, institutional structures, social interaction patterns, and processes. The difficult next step is to gather in-depth information on the community structure. Details such as mapping the major elements and processes of the social system are critical to determining what the *real* problems are and how the system might be alerted to resolve them. During this phase the practitioner obtains data on the beliefs, goals, roles, norms, and sanctions in the community and relevant information on the power structure, influence system, and shared community goals (Blakely, 1972). Collecting this information might involve a variety of techniques from sociology and anthropology, such as participant observations combined with structured interviews. These methods usually yield the richest data in such inquiries. In addition to gaining information on the who and what of this social system, the how questions must be answered. These are the process issues such as communication, decision making, client boundary maintenance, institutionalization, or socialization that maintains the inertia of the socioeconomic order.

Warren (1965), in his classic work on community development, *Studying Your Community,* provides one of the most detailed approaches to this type of in-depth community analysis. Krammer (1960), in *The Diagnostic Process in Adult Education,* emphasizes the importance of linking the diagnostic process to the community situation. These scholars and other practitioners recognize that the perceived needs or general community interest are only part of the total picture in analyzing the community situation. From these data the practitioner should identify a set of "generative themes" (World Education, 1973), that is, a series of topics that reflect the specific problems that arise in the context of the community's day-to-day activities. A generative theme has both individual and group significance. For example, a desire for self-respect might be a common individual response in a community where there is a general racial or ethnic injustice. The factors that might increase individual self-esteem in this situation might be identified in the community as jobs, housing, health, and the like. Therefore, the community education practitioner must assist in developing a program that addresses itself to the individual's needs for self-identity by providing resources for employment opportunities and better housing. However, the social structure must be modified to accommodate the rising expectations of the target population. A program that develops jobs for the target population without providing increased social opportunities will inevitably contribute to intensified community animosities. Therefore, the diagnostician must be acquainted with how all parts of the system relate to one another and the impact that altering any of its parts has on the whole. This will be discussed later in greater detail.

TENTATIVE INTERVENTION DESIGN AND TRIAL INTERVENTIONS

Social intervention theory is not as well developed as the clinical intervention theory in fields such as psychology, psychiatry, and medicine. Nonetheless, social practitioners are involved in constructing interventions in community life that frequently have permanent effects. For instance, welfare, public housing, and unemployment insurance were not envisioned at their introduction to be of the size and scope they are today. Frequently community development interventions bring some permanent or fixed institutional arrangements from evening schools to community centers. Many of these programs continue beyond their original purposes without the means to change. Consequently, some early assessment must be made of the potential short- and long-range effects of the new program.

Developing and testing of a variety of intervention strategies has the benefit of (1) ascertaining whether the intervention will work, (2) determining the parts of the community and/or client system it affects, and (3) finding out, to the extent possible, the long-range implications of the particular strategy for budget and other resources.

Each generative theme should be explored with a series of experimental interventions. Interventions can and should be tested using a variety of approaches. This might include developing miniprojects in the target area for a short period to test the strategy. Other methods such as simulations, sampling, or even "attitude reactionaires" (questionnaires to test response to a new program) might be employed. However, a test trial or dry run should usually precede the introduction of the new program. David Harmon's work in literacy and family planning for World Education (1973) provides one of the clearest explanations of intervention design strategies. Harmon's book offers a practical blueprint for the practitioner in developing a "situation specific" intervention strategy. The first step is an intervention strategy developed for particular problems of the community as opposed to national or regional approaches.

DIAGNOSTIC EVALUATION

Evaluation is part of the total feedback system at every level in education and development. Consequently, evaluation is necessarily included in the diagnostic model. The practitioner must be certain that he or she is attacking the correct problem and has identified the best intervention for the specific target population. In some instances, excellent programs have not succeeded because of failure to consider whether the program was designed for the appropriate target population. A recent illustration of this problem is the family planning programs of West Africa and the Caribbean. The original "sex education" aspects of family life were designed for teenage women. However, it was soon discovered that *grandmothers* transmitted most, if not all, sex information to teenagers. When several of the programs were revamped on early diagnostic evaluation of the correct population, grandmothers were involved, with excellent results.

Diagnostic evaluation is best accomplished with the assistance of outside experts and potential program participants. The outsiders can provide insights into the data that those closely involved might overlook. Furthermore, potential participants can assist in telling the sponsors whether the idea makes any sense. The participant diagnostic evaluation process is based on the concepts developed by Strauss, Glasser, (1967) of "fit" and "work." In essence, do the data *fit* or describe the actual situation and will the intervention work if applied to this unique situation?

DIAGNOSIS, EDUCATION, AND BEHAVIORAL CHANGE

The analytical base for examining sociocultural systems is composed of three components: ideology, technology, and organization (LaBelle, 1973). Ideology is the value orientation of the community (nature, God, basic beliefs about humanity, etc.). Technology is the community's use of material resources, from bricks to energy. Organization refers to how people in the community bring themselves together for governance or social order. LaBelle points out that no intended alteration of any one component can take place unless one of the others is altered by the same or a related intervention strategy. In other words, people will not adopt new practices unless, for example, their belief system supports it. Using family planning as an illustration, it is well known that the introduction of birth control methods cannot succeed without major alterations in the belief system. Therefore, diagnostic inquiry and analysis of intervention strategies is related directly to the problem as well as to the supporting components. LaBelle theorizes that "there exist only three points of intervention through which change can occur and intervention must be made simultaneously in more than one in order to increase the probability that the intended change will be manifested" (LaBelle, 1973, p. 25). An example of this process might be assisting a community with its health problems through the construction of a clinic (technology) run by a local board of directors (organizational) in order to provide modern health care, with the assistance of the local religious leaders (ideological). The diagnostic methodology here is focused on the diffusion process (education) and its impacts on institutional and social arrangements (behavioral). This model moves away from diagnosis as simply the discovery of the current status of a behavioral system. Diagnostic methods are part of the tactics of introducing change. Previously, the diagnostic system was discussed as a means to explore alternatives and to identify the stimulus for or barriers to change. Here diagnosis or needs analysis is used as a means to develop the mechanisms for behavioral change. The focal point in the change process is the educational strategy. There is a community educational link for each of the sociocultural components (technology, organization, and ideology). The diagnostic method can identify an appropriate educational strategy appropriate to the particular situation. Community education in this context becomes the catalyst for behavioral modification. Therefore, the educational efforts should be an integral part of *the tentative intervention* design.

In this model, *education is not the end in itself, but the vehicle to a total community behavioral modification.* By combining our earlier discussions on diagnostic phases with the components of the sociocultural system, an interesting and useful matrix emerges. (Figure 7–1)

This matrix provides the field practitioner with a handy analytical framework for the diagnostic evaluation process. Displaying the data in this way is also helpful in orienting community school staff, board members, laypersons, educators, and others to the project. It translates the complex systems data into a manageable form easily understood by persons familiar with community development work.

CASE STUDY—APPLYING THE DIAGNOSTIC SYSTEM

The five-step diagnostic method described in this chapter should be used with flexibility. It is designed to suggest a systematic and useful approach for the field practitioner in assembling the required information for program design.

Many successful projects have intuitively used the system described in this chapter without elaborate data-gathering or information analysis devices. This system is essentially a qualitative instead of a quantitative technique. Although the number of persons of various age, sex, ethnicity, or other numerical information is essential, the field study should concentrate on the intensity of the local persons' aspirations to attain certain deeply felt needs. A questionnaire or interview may help to yield these data, but several projects have used unique means to obtain important information on the goals, the communities, and their problems and internal organization. In the following two case studies, specific means were used to diagnose local needs.

Figure 7-1   Diagnosis evaluation matrix.

Component

Phase	Technology	Organization	Ideology	Community development strategy
1. Prediagnosis (first impression)	(Information)--------→			Current status
2. Diagnostic entry (detailed data gathering)	(Information)--------→			
3. Tentative intervention design (experimental methods)	(Responses)--------→			Develop, design, and test new non-formal education methods
4. Trial interventions (field test)	(Responses)--------→			
5. Diagnostic evaluation (interpretation)	(Responses)--------→			Evaluation of development strategy with total intervention model

Family Life Education in Turkey (Case 1)

Turkey, like many developing countries, is introducing mass literacy programs to improve citizen awareness and agricultural and industrial productivity. Adult literacy has been part of modern Turkey since the days of Ataturk. However, adult literacy in Turkey, as in many developing nations, was based on the traditional literacy primer. The primers themselves were relatively well written and included adult-oriented stories and pictures. However, there was no real incentive for an adult to labor through the primer to learn to read. The Turkish government, in collaboration with World Education, launched a project in July 1971 in an effort to stimulate greater participation in literacy programs. Unlike the earlier endeavors, the Turkish government and World Education agreed that the adults' learning needs, interest, and learning styles would form the basis of whatever literacy program was designed.

Five provinces were selected for an analysis of adult literacy needs. The diagnostic process commenced with visits to the provinces by trained adult education specialists. These specialists were to listen to conversations of local farmers, workers, and other illiterates and determine what they talked about most and why. This information was noted or tape-recorded and combined with unstructured interviews with a cross section of local people on the general problems of the area. Analysis of the information in each province revealed certain patterns or themes and specific key words used repeatedly in reference to local situation. Each of these generative themes was then researched in greater depth through interviews, observations, and further collection of important words or phrases. To aid in the in-depth analysis, sketches were developed depicting common local scenes. These drawings were shown to local people to stimulate discussions with individuals and groups. The information regarding the responses to the sketches was tabulated along with the other data.

Subsequent to the analysis of the data, experimental literacy sessions were developed to pretest the methods and materials with local illiterates in each village. Pictures and words developed in the earlier surveys were used. The responses indicated that the local sketches, which related to local agricultural production, health practices, and civic problems, stimulated lively discussions and a subsequent high recall of the written words associated with the lessons. The curriculum was then devised from the diagnostic evaluation based on the following points.

1. Pictures are more attractive than words, particularly to illiterates.
2. Illiterates can learn to read pictures more easily than words.
3. Reading a series of connected pictures as a unified story is a useful preliminary to reading a series of connected words.
4. Illiterates' behavior can be modified toward modern agriculture and health practice while the individual gains literacy skills.
5. The literacy training class or group forms a new social group in which individual as well as collective change is encouraged and supported.

This entire process took nearly a year, but the resultant literacy-family life project was extremely successful. Literacy was the community education vehicle for agricultural and family life information. Functional literacy provided the cornerstone of the diffusion process to modify the entire community structure. Improved farm practice (technology) supported altered family life practices (ideology) and helped to develop new responses to national development goals through the literacy classes (organization).

A Pilot Project in New Jersey Adult Basic Education

East Orange is not Turkey, but it nonetheless has literacy problems. In fact, some of the functionally illiterate in East Orange have attended school. Many, of course, were drop-outs, while others attended schools in Puerto Rico, the South, or outside the United States.

In New Jersey the problem was to identify a means to reach the functionally illiterate so they could enter the job market or move up the job ladder. Clearly, telling someone who had been to school that he or she was not literate would only damage egos without altering the situation. Therefore, the Adult Basic Education Project devised a project to assist adults to gain vocational skills while completing high school diplomas or vocational training requirements. Prior to developing the project, a diagnostic inventory was conducted in the area similar to the one described earlier (Turkey). However, instead of taking notes, tape recordings of conversations in bars, restaurants, and homes were used to generate the significant issues in the community.

These data were analyzed together with local citizens' reactions to photographs taken of ordinary street scenes. Each respondent was asked what the picture meant to him or her and how it related to the community. The information was summarized for each picture that consistently brought forth similar reactions. These photographs together with information on the community, local language patterns, and other data were transformed into easy-to-read stories at the fourth- through the eighth-grade level. The pictures and stories became part of the Adult Basic Education Program as civics and family life information, not as literacy. Literacy in this example is the technology that is being used to alter the ideology (feeling of helplessness and low self-esteem) and use the class as a civic action group (organization).

Conclusion

There are many diagnostic strategies applicable in any development context. The attempt here is to merge the methodologies of three overlapping social technologies in community development into a coherent and intelligent system that is easily applied in most situations.

This methodology has the advantage of being systematic without being rigid. It can be used or modified in any setting by a field practitioner. Hopefully, community workers or others working in community situations will expand on this model.

BIBLIOGRAPHY AND REFERENCES

Blakely, E. J. *Training people for the war on poverty.* New York: Vantage, 1972.

Center for Research on Utilization of Scientific Knowledge (CRUSK)—Institute for Social Research. The University of Michigan, Ann Arbor, Michigan, 1972. The Center prepares many useful papers on organizational change that have applicability to most community change situations as well.

Famer, J., Sheats, P., & Deshler, D. An Evaluation of Title I (HEA, 1965) Program in California, 1966–71. The California Coordinating Council of Higher Education, 1972.

Krammer, C. *The diagnostic process in adult education.* Bloomington, Ind. Indiana University, 1960.

LaBelle, T. Social and cultural change. University of California, Los Angeles, unpublished mimeo, 1973.

Lippitt, R., Watson, J., & Westley, B. *The dynamics of planned change.* New York: Harcourt-Brace, 1958.

McMahon, E. *Needs—of people and their communities and the adult educator.* Washington, D.C.: American Adult Education Association, 1970.

Rice, A. K. *Productivity and social organization—the ahmedabad experiment.* London: Tavistock Institute, 1958.

Sanders, I. The community social profile. *American Sociological Review,* 1960, **XXV** (1), 75–77.

Seashore, S. E., & Bowers, D. C. Durability of organizational change. *American Psychologist,* 1970, **75,** 227–233.

Strauss, A., Glaser, B. *The discovery of grounded theory.* Chicago: Aldine Publishers, 1967.

Warren, R. *Studying your community.* New York: The Free Press, 1965.

Chapter 8

PROBLEMS IN THE EVALUATION OF COMMUNITY DEVELOPMENT EFFORTS

Donald E. Voth

WHY ENGAGE IN EVALUATION?

Why should we attempt to evaluate community development efforts? The answer is not as obvious as it might seem, when we consider two facts. First, systematic evaluation of the effects of major social programs is very recent (Wholey et al., 1971). Very little systematic evaluation was done of New Deal programs in the 1930s, and the efforts that were begun were abandoned when the social programs were abandoned, either because of a rightwing reaction to them or because World War II apparently brought an end to the problems they were intended to alleviate. Second, Community development is viewed by at least some of its practitioners as a kind of existential activity; each group, each community, has unique goals, and the community development professional is there to help them reach these unique goals. Consequently, it is impossible to isolate any general objectives. This, of course, precludes most types of evaluation. Indeed, within this view of community development one finds evaluation frequently meaning quite a different thing from the way I will define it shortly, to refer to the more or less continuous personal feedback of participants regarding their perception of the process.

However, the obvious answer to the original question is still the most important. We need to know whether or not community development efforts have any of the effects they are proported to have, we need to know how these effects are brought about, and we need to know why they are not brought about if they are unsuccessful. Finally, we need to know something about the relationship between their costs and benefits so that we can make intelligent choices among alternatives.

There is one other reason that, while perhaps not as important as these, is still significant. We are in need of greater understanding of the community development process in order to train a new generation of community development practitioners. The fact is that community development practice, as it exists today, is more like an art than a science, more something you are born with and not something you learn systematically, partly because we cannot generalize about the process whereby groups and communities grow and develop.

Finally, and perhaps most compelling, is the fact that "accountability" is the watchword these days. We will be evaluated, whether we want to be or not. Hence we are well advised to take care that evaluation is as sensitive and accurate as possible.

SOME DEFINITIONS

In order to delineate the universe of discourse, let me define roughly what I mean by community development and evaluation. When I talk about community development, I refer to a situation in which some group, usually locality based, such as a neighborhood or local community, attempts to improve its social and economic situation through its own efforts with professional assistance and perhaps also financial assistance from the outside, and with maximum involvement of all sectors of the community or group. None of these characteristics, taken by themselves, are essential to the definition. For example, a community development program can be initiated from the outside instead of from inside the community. What my definition does require is that most of the characteristics be present. This style of community development is most thoroughly described by Poston (1953) in *Democracy is You,* by Sanders (1953) in *Making Good Communities Better,* and by Bruyn (1963) in his comparative study of two slightly different styles of community development in *Communities in Action: Pattern and Process.* It is also used by the Chamber of Commerce of the United States (1968) in their community development programs, as expressed in their *Forward Thrust: Guidelines for Mobilizing Total Community Resources.*

These projects typically involve the formation of communitywide steering committees, the execution of one or several surveys of community needs and priorities, usually by community people themselves, and the formation of numerous study and action committees to deal with various aspects of community life (housing, health and health services, education, etc.). These projects may last from 6 months to 2 years or more, with great emphasis being placed on citizen participation in committees, task forces, and town meetings.

Evaluation research, or "evaluative" research, according to Suchman (1967, p. 7), is fundamentally the same as basic social science research as one finds it presented by the standard texts of research methodology and as one finds it practiced by researchers. The major difference is in the variables involved. Evaluation research is concerned with policy-relevant variables, at least some of which are manipulable, and not with the generic concepts that underlie those variables. These policy-relevant variables normally include at least one that represents the existence or nonexistence of some kind of social program, or some kind of treatment that is alleged to have certain predictable effects. This variable can, of course, take more than just two values; for example, one may be concerned about the differential effects of four, or eight or any number of different "treatments."

Furthermore, evaluation research, as I will discuss it here, necessarily involves comparison. This may mean comparison of what happens to one unit during a series of time intervals, as in time series analysis, or more commonly, comparison of a large number of units over roughly the same time interval. Thus evaluation research will normally involve delineating a population of communities (or groups), sampling from those communities (or groups), and in some way measuring each of the samples on a wide range of variables, including the major treatment variable and the major effect variable. Inferences are then made to the larger population of units with conventional inferential statistics and using tests of significance. In some instances the total population of units will be analyzed, (e.g., all of the counties in a state), so that problems of inference do not arise.

There are five problems in the evaluation of community development efforts that I will discuss. The first two are conceptual problems, the next two are technical problems, and the last is actually a whole set of political problems. They are as follows.

1. Ambiguity of goals in community development.
2. Absence of a model of the community development process.

3. Inability of the researcher to control assignment to treatments.
4. Weak effects, crude measurement, and small samples.
5. Political problems—the relationship between evaluation and program administration.

Ambiguity of Goals in Community Development

The goals of community development are usually vague, contradictory, and evanescent. Of course, this should not surprise us. After all, who knows the goals of our schools, of higher education, of local governments, or of the extension service, the university, or the experiment stations? General statements abound, but clear operational definitions on which we would be willing to stake our jobs and our reputations are amazingly hard to come by, and not only for community development. These institutions are all alike and are similar to community development in that their goals are very general, appear as vague abstractions, and are extremely complex. It is a major rule of evaluation that the goals of the activity to be evaluated must be stated in clear operational terms before evaluation can even be seriously considered (Suchman, 1967, pp. 37, 38). Thus we have our first dilemma.

It is helpful to understand some of the reasons for the ambiguity of goals in community development. Perhaps the most important has to do with politics; this is a problem not only for community development, but for most social programs that in any way owe their existence to the political process. To serve their political function, the objectives of such programs must be ambitious (eliminate poverty), very general, and acceptable to everyone. This almost guarantees that their pretentions will exceed their capabilities, especially when they are funded at the low levels at which social programs have been funded recently. It also guarantees that they will be subject to contradictory interpretations by different parties and that they will not be stated in operational terms.*

Another point of difficulty is in the distinction between what are frequently referred to as "process" and "content" objectives. "Content" objectives are the concrete, frequently physical, results of community development activity (water systems, parks, a new school, etc.); "process" objectives are the ability of the community to solve its problems and to make decisions collectively. Hence the process objectives imply collective changes in behavior. It is frequently held that, while the content objectives can, in principle, be measured, the process objectives cannot, and thus conventional evaluation techniques cannot be applied to community development. A very similar objection to evaluation states that community development usually seeks to achieve institutional change instead of simply aggregating changes in the behaviors of individuals, and that institutional change can only be measured by "qualitative methods" instead of by conventional comparative techniques (Weiss & Rein, 1972). Although neither of these positions is valid as stated, they indicate the need for clarity in the objectives with respect to the level (individual, family, group, neighborhood, community, etc.), which is the primary target of community development programs, and the development of measurement techniques appropriate for those levels.

Now the evaluator must have community development goals stated in operational terms. Furthermore, unless there is consensus on goals beforehand, to quote Weiss (1972):

*For an excellent discussion of what happens to social programs in the political process see Marris and Rein (1969).

• program decision-makers can later dismiss results of even the best evaluation study by saying, "but that's not what we were trying to do." If an evaluation of a preschool program shows that pupils did not learn verbal and numerical concepts, program advocates can claim that they were improving the children's medical and dental care or creating positive attitudes in parents toward the school. (p. 7)

I suppose the obvious solution is for the evaluator to fold his or her hands and wait for program administrators to come forward with the objectives to be measured. However, if the evaluator takes this position, he or she should, as Freeman and Sherwood have suggested, ". . . bring lots of novels to the office to read while he waits" (Weiss, 1972, p. 21).

Thus the researcher has no alternative to becoming actively involved in the specification of goals, in identifying which goals are held by which parties to the program,* and in developing empirical measures of these goals.

LACK OF A CAUSAL MODEL OF THE COMMUNITY DEVELOPMENT PROCESS

Ideally we would be able to lay out in the order of their respective causes and effects the components of the community development process. That we cannot do so is one of the major impediments to evaluation. We can look to the Community Action Programs, as well as several other components of the Economic Opportunity legislation of 1964, for an example of what such a model would look like. Although I do not advocate this particular model, the fact that programs were designed in accordance with a theoretical model of how poverty should be attacked is commendable.

*For an excellent discussion of the delineation of the different goals held by different parties interested in social programs see Borus and Tash (1970).

On the basis of experience in the Ford Foundation's "Gray Areas" programs of the 1950s and certain theoretical notions about the genesis of juvenile delinquency (Merton, 1957; Cloward & Ohlin, 1960), it was felt that the solution to poverty was to be found in community action, that is, in local people becoming involved in solving their own problems, and that the proper role of outside agencies like the Ford Foundation and eventually the federal government was to nurture such organization and involvement.

Vanecko et al. (1970) have summarized the approach as follows.

> The theoretical basis of the Community Action Program is built on the proposition that poverty in an affluent society is not the result of the inability of individuals to obtain and control economic resources, but instead is the result of the inability of groups of poor people to obtain and exercise sufficient control over institutions that serve them, or should serve them. The theory states that unless people have enough power to exert some influence over the institutions that affect their lives, they will not participate in those institutions, will not benefit from the resources that those institutions offer and will become detached from the social system (or alienated). Thus, the existence of poverty as a social problem is a matter neither of lack of individual economic resources nor of simple "relative deprivation" but of removal from the poor of control over institutions that serve them. The theory states that this power vacuum has come about in a wide variety of ways, such as the increasing scale of society, the elimination of ethnic politics and/or urban political bosses, and the concentration of the black poor population in the northern urban ghettoes. However, the critical fact is that all of these processes together are producing an increasing detachment on the part of the poor population and thus are intensifying the cycle of poverty. Both power itself and self-awareness of power are necessary. (p. 2)

A relatively simple theoretical statement such as this sets the stage for developing a model of how the problem is to be solved. For example, increase in local political power by the poor is one of the obvious objectives and a prime candidate for measurement of the success or failure of the program. The model also suggests that these increases should lead to decreases in alienation and in actual movement out of poverty as local institutions become more responsive to the needs of the poor. It also suggests points at which the problem can be attacked, the "policy variables" in the system. Organization of the poor can be stimulated and the poor can be employed in positions of responsibility in local agencies and institutions in order to give them control of these institutions.

The crucial point for our purposes is that such a model specifies both the target of the program (poor neighborhoods as social systems), the ultimate objective or objectives (alleviation of poverty), and the intermediate objectives (increase political power of poor), in their order of causation.

Thus the model serves as a guide to the evaluator in designing his or her research. It specifies the target of the program, which should, of course, also be the unit of analysis for the measurement of effects.* It specifies what should be correlated with what in what causal order so that an in-depth evaluation can detect not only whether or not a program had an impact, but where in the causal chain the process broke down if the expected impact did not occur. It suggests where to look for undesirable side effects. It also suggests where proxy measures are to be found for crucial variables if these variables cannot be measured directly. Finally, it is the basic groundwork for the essential decision rules in evaluation.

*This elementary point seems to be rediscovered again and again in the social sciences. See, for example, Lazarsfeld and Menzel (1961) and, quite recently, Lineberry (1971), who go over the same ground. For my purposes it suffices to insist that community development should be evaluated at the level of the community and not at the level of individuals, families, the region, or the nation.

We do have some abstract models of the community development process. F. W. Young and his associates at Cornell University have for a number of years worked on a model for which the unit of analysis is the community as a social system and for which the crucial variables are community differentiation or complexity, community solidarity, and community articulation, or centrality in the system of communities (Young & Young, 1974). The abstractness of this model, however, makes it difficult to apply in the evaluation of community development as it is actually practiced in the field. When it is applied, the things that are measured are not the things that practitioners themselves feel they are trying to achieve.

The first two problems, then, are basically problems in the conceptualization of the community development process: (1) objectives are usually vague, and (2) there is no clearly articulated causal model of how these objectives are to be brought about.

The next two problems are essentially technical problems in evaluation research.

Inability of the Researcher to Control Assignment to Experimental and Control Groups

My underlying approach to evaluation is experimental design, and it depends heavily on the work of Campbell (Cambell & Stanley, 1966). The essential feature of experimental design is that it solves a major problem of internal validity in a uniquely efficient manner. The problem is that variables other than the treatment variable may actually be responsible for effects that are observed in a scientific study. In experimental design, subjects (communities) are assigned to treatment and control groups randomly in order to eliminate all of these alternative explanations at one time.

To illustrate, suppose we have a program designed to increase citizen participation in community decision making. We decide to assign community development practitioners to use certain specified techniques that are supposed to increase citizen participation. We will send practitioners to some communities and refrain from sending them to others, so that we can use the latter communities as controls. Our expectation is, of course, that citizen participation will improve more in those that have the community development practitioners than in those that do not; this is our research hypothesis.

These communities will, of course, differ on a wide range of characteristics, some of which, no doubt, have an influence on their subsequent improvement in citizen participation. If we allow communities to select themselves into the experimental and control groups, it is almost certain that the experimentals and controls would not be equivalent on these other variables or, to say the same thing in a different way, that there would be a correlation between the experimental variable and some of these other variables. Hence we cannot tell, if there are any effects of program, whether these effects are due to the program or to the preexisting values on these other variables. We are not likely to be better off if program administrators make the selection. They will usually select those that they know, probably in the basis of these "other" variables, to have a better chance of succeeding—unless, of course, they want the experiment to fail, in which case they will do the opposite. In both cases our "experiment" does not have internal vailidity; that is, it cannot logically give an unequivocal answer to our research question. The observed effects are due either to the program, to these other variables, or to both, but we cannot say which is the case.

Random assignment is an ingenious way of assuring that there is no correlation between the treatment variable and all of these other variables, including all of those we have not yet thought of. Hence, in the true experiment, one can simply forget about them.

It is clear that we will seldom be able to control the assignment of community development programs. Campbell has coined the term "quasiexperiments" for research in real-world situations that in some respects approximate experiments, but in which some crucial feature of the experiment is not feasible (Campbell & Stanley, 1966, p. 34). He then proceeds to apply the logic of experimental design to these situations and suggests a number of quasiexperimental designs that are appropriate under different circumstances. His major contribution is that the logic of experimental design gives us a systematic way of detecting weakness in specific quasiexperiments.

The major problem with the design of the above example is that selection to experimental and control groups is not random; thus we cannot eliminate alternative causal explanations in wholesale fashion. The solution is to anticipate these alternative causes, to measure them explicitly, and thus to incorporate them into our model. Therefore, if we had reason to believe that preexisting levels of citizen participation were the real cause of observed effects of programs (those that started at higher levels were more likely to increase), and that explained both selection to program and improvements in citizen participation, we would need to control for the effects of citizen participation by examining the differences between experimental and control groups within different levels of prior citizen participation. The test of our hypothesis is simply whether, when controlling for all of these other variables, there is any net difference between experimental and control groups.

However, if the correlation between the treatment variable and prior citizen participation is too great, this controlled analysis cannot be performed; within a given level of citizen participation there would be only either experimental communities or control communities. The solution to this is apparently to move back slightly toward the pure experiment and, by anticipating alternative explanatory variables and their probable correlations with the crucial experimental variable, to persuade program administrators at least to select a few communities in each of a set of categories generated by cross classifying the experimental variables and these alternative variables. In terms of our above example this would mean to try to select at least a few communities in each of four types: (1) high participation with the community development program, (2) high participation without the program, (3) low participation with the program, and (4) low participation without the program. Since more than one alternative explanatory variable is proposed this procedure demands considerable prior knowledge of the intercorrelations among the relevant variables.

Moving from experimental design to dynamic causal models such as this has certain advantages in addition to the fact that it is frequently the only thing that is feasible. By incorporating more than one stage of the causal process onto the analysis, it lends itself to a fuller exploration of the total process whereby community development occurs. If self-selection to programs is a fact of life, it may be better to understand the exact role it plays than to ignore it, providing that, by attempting to do so, one does not jeopardize answering the major research question. It also lends itself more readily to changes in the design of the experiment while it is being carried out—and this is a serious problem in evaluating social programs. Program administrators, quite intelligently, look for feedback and alter programs in midstream on the basis of such feedback. A true experimental design may be jeopardized by such changes, whereas the dynamic causal model we are suggesting here may simply require the incorporation of an additional variable. Thus this model is much more capable of comprehending the social programming process as it actually occurs.*

The dynamic causal model also has disadvantages. The most serious is its inability to rule out all alternative causal explanations at one time. It can, at best, rule out only those that are anticipated and are explicitly incorporated into this model, and even then only when these alternative variables taken individually or as a group are not so highly correlate with the treatment variable that no significant variation remains in the treatment variable.*

Another problem with the dynamic causal model as a substitute for true experimental design is sampling. If we wish to eliminate or minimize the correlation between the treatment variable and several alternative causal variables, we may find ourselves with many types from which to sample. This implies, of course, the need for larger and larger samples as the number of intercorrelated variables increases. Furthermore, we may not know what these intercorrelations are; indeed, we may not even know the values of these variables for the population at the time that our sample is drawn.

It should be obvious by now that the existence of a clearly articulated model of the community development process greatly enhances one's ability to indentify plausible alternatives and thus to apply a causal evaluation model.

WEAK EFFECTS, CRUDE MEASUREMENT, AND SMALL SAMPLES

Community development efforts cannot be expected to have dramatic effects, at least not at the levels that they

---

*For a fuller development of these ideas see Hawkes (1974), on whom this section is based.

*This is the problem of multicollinearity. Even a rudimentary discussion of this problem as it appears in the literature on multiple correlation and regression is beyond the scope of this chapter.

have been supported in the past. One professional operating in a district of from six to eight counties cannot expect to revolutionize his or her area, especially when you consider the relationship of this or her efforts to all of the aggregate energy that is normally expanded. Furthermore, community development frequently has subtle goals that, to be realized, require changes of behavior for large numbers of people or the alteration of major institutions in the community. Compared to the other influences on those people and on those institutions, the efforts of community development practitioners are infinitesimal. To be sure, some of the justification for community development is that it has a high multiplier effect, that is, that the community developer stimulates changes that, in turn, stimulate further changes far in excess of the original energy invested. In fact, one of the justifications for community action in the Office of Economic Opportunity (OEO) was that money spent in mobilizing the poor would result in greater benefits to the people in the target neighborhoods than merely channeling the funds directly to the intended recipients (Vanecko et al., 1970, pp. 5, 6). Nevertheless, most community development activities cannot realistically be expected to have dramatic effects.

Furthermore, the goals of community development can usually be measured only very crudely. There are no good sensitive measures of the distribution of influence or power in community decision making, or of something like the quality of life in communities.

Finally, the targets of community development efforts are usually groups or whole communities. Thus samples must really be taken from a population of groups or communities, not from populations of individuals within a community. However, to measure a variable at the group or community level, it may be necessary, further, to sample the individuals within it, so what one gets is a kind of cluster sample in which the clusters of individuals represent only one sample of the primary unit of analysis. Obviously this is costly, since it reduces the sample sizes.

To some extent the size of the effects expected, the precision of the measurement, and the size of samples are substitutable. That is, if your samples must be small, you can opt for a more precise measurement device and still have a reasonably powerful research design. In the evaluation of community development, one has nothing to substitute.

POLITICAL PROBLEMS OF EVALUATION

Implicit in much of the discussion so far has been the conflict or strain, at least potential conflict or strain, between the research and the research team on the one hand and program administrators and those who carry out the programs on the other. Thus, it was suggested earlier that the research would need to obtain a commitment from program administrators to specific operational measures of program effects to avoid the possibility that, once the research results are available, program administrators disclaim the measures actually used. The major point to be made here is that the goals and objectives of any program serve different functions to different people. Although it would be a mistake to imply that politicians are less concerned with "objective" results than academics, it is, nevertheless, true that at certain points in the career of any major social program the goals are much more important to politicians as symbols to be used to appeal to the voting public than as objective statements of what the programs actually will accomplish. Vague, abstract, and uncontroversial goal statements are required for this function, just the opposite of what is required for effective program evaluation. In fact, the person who engages in evaluation research soon learns that evaluation itself serves many different functions to many different people, and that if the evaluator is not careful, he or she may be "used" for some partisan purpose that was not anticipated (Morris & Rein, 1969).

A more specific source of conflict between evaluators and administrators is that the latter are eager to obtain ongoing feedback in order to improve programs, whereas the former frequently view this as diluting the experiment and prefer to wait until the procedure has run its course before looking at the data. This points to the need to distinguish between at least two types of evaluation with a view to perhaps finding different organizational niches for each (Wholey et al., 1971, p. 25). They are impact evaluation and strategy evaluation. Impact evaluation is concerned with determining whether or not a program has effects, what kinds of effects it has or, perhaps, of comparing the effects of two programs. Ideally, impact evaluation should be independent of program administration in order to give it both the substance and the appearance of objectivity and to free the program administrator from the responsibility of supervising the activity that may result in the demise of his or her program. Impact evaluation frequently generates considerable controversy, and occasionally results in debates about esoteric statistical procedures in the media, as was the case with the Head Start study and the Coleman Report on education in the United States (Weiss, 1972, p. 327).

Strategy evaluation is the comparative assessment of different techniques or approaches applied by a particular agency. A good example of strategy evaluation is the National Opinion Research Center's evaluation of the Community Action Programs (CAP) of the Office of Economic Opportunity (OEO) (Vanecko et al., 1970). In this evaluation the issue was whether CAP's emphasis on community organization and mobilization was more likely to influence local institutions than the emphasis of other agencies on a service strategy. Needless to say, this research was not a serious threat to OEO as a whole, and it was performed under OEO supervision.*

However, rearrangement of administrative location of evaluative research cannot eliminate the fact that between program administration and program evaluation of any kind there is an adversary relationship. In strategy evaluation, although there may be no conflict with top program administration, lower levels of administration will represent different strategies that are, presumably, being compared. Each will have at least some investment in seeing its strategy proven effective. If this commitment does not exist, it is quite certain that it will *not* be effective. Consequently, the research operation will still be a threat to someone. Certainly the research operation cannot be under the exclusive control of the people or divisions that are under threat, but to separate them administratively results in communication difficulties. Thus you have a dilemma. The research operation needs to be administratively autonomous enough to protect its objectivity, but it needs to be close enough to the "nitty-gritty" of program operation to be able to obtain the information and insights that are required for a sensitive evaluation.

The solution, to some people, is improved human relations, improved risktaking capabilities on the part of program administrators, and increased empathy on the part of researchers. I doubt that this is very promising. I believe it is far better to depend on research design to solve these problems; the key is in the prior explication of program objectives at all levels, of operational measures of these objectives acceptable to both program administration and researchers, and of the decision rules to be used in analyzing these operational measures and anticipating their consequences. Then research, when it actually gets underway,

---

*Unfortunately, strategy evaluation is frequently billed, implicitly at least, as impact evaluation. See, for example, Clark and Hopkins (1969).

is more or less a mechanical procedure allowing a minimum of discretionary intervention by either researchers or program administrators.

Another political problem in the area of evaluation research is the utilization of research results. It was common several years ago to deplore the fact that research results were not used by administrators anyway. I really doubt that this is true in the area of social programming anymore. Indeed, the opposite may be true; too much reliance may be placed on research that is either technically defective or that attempts to evaluate processes that are so complicated and subtle that they cannot be adequately assessed with the research techniques available. I suggest that the "culture of poverty" is an example of an area where the latter is true. The concept is so vague that its components cannot be operationalized. Consequently policy and evaluation of policy based on the idea of the culture of poverty are both bound to be inconclusive; however, this did not discourage us from designing programs based on that concept during the 1960s.

At least in one respect there is a problem of utilization; as pointed out, program administrators need ongoing feedback and evaluators are frequently reluctant or unable to supply it. When the evaluators' results do become available, the national mood has taken a different turn and the legislation has either been scrapped or expanded without the benefit of the insight that the research might have provided. Here, as stated previously, a more dynamic system model of evaluation might contribute to the utilization of results and thereby to better communication between administrators and evaluators.

Finally, the majority of careful evaluations of social programs emanating out of the activist 1960s have apparently shown that these programs have had very minor effects or no effect at all. I have observed the same thing with community development activities that I studied in southern Illinois (Voth, 1975). I, personally, am not sure just what to make of this preponderance of null results. Weiss (1972, p. 366) has discussed the issue briefly but well, and there is no need to repeat her discussion. I do suggest that the community developer or the administrator of a community development program who is anticipating an evaluation take this fact into consideration. Your evaluation could be a thorn in your side and could deny that your program is accomplishing anything when you know intuitively and on the basis of common opinion that you are having at least some effects.

A Concluding Suggestion

One strategy that promises to ameliorate several of the problems of evaluation research has not yet been mentioned. It is more systematic cumulation and use of secondary data on communities. What is being suggested is the careful aggregation of social indicators at the community level (Rossi, 1972). The suggestion is not new. However, those of us who work with small communities and nonmetropolitan areas are still awaiting the fruits of recent developments in social indicators, large-scale data archiving, and the like. One of the most serious impediments to developments in this area is the "project approach to social science research, which does not encourage cumulative data archiving.

BIBLIOGRAPHY AND REFERENCES

Borus, M. E., & Tash, W. R. *Measuring the impact of manpower programs: A primer.* Ann arbor: Institute of Labor and Industrial Relations, The University of Michigan-Wayne State University, 1970.

Bruyn, S. T. *Communities in action: Pattern and process.* New Haven, Conn.: College and University Press, 1963.

Chamber of Commerce of the United States. Forward Thrust: Guidelines for Mobilizing Total Community Resources. Washington, DC 1968.

Campbell, D. T., & Stanley, J. C. *Experimental and quasi-experimental designs for research.* Chicago: Rand McNally, 1966.

Caro, F. G. (Ed.) *Readings in evaluation research.* New York: Russell Sage Foundation, 1971.

Clark, K., & Hopkins, J. *A relevant war against poverty: A study of community action programs and observable social change.* New York: Harper and Row, 1969.

Cloward, R., & Ohlin, L. E. *Delinquency and opportunity: A theory of delinquent gangs.* New York: Free Press, 1960.

Hawkes, R. K. Structural equations in evaluational research. Carbondale, Ill: Department of Sociology, Southern Illinois University (mimeo). Paper read at an institute on Methodological Concerns in Evaluational Research at Loyola University, Chicago, May 31, 1974.

Lazarsfeld, P. F., & Menzel, H. On the relation between individual and collective properties. In Amitai Etzioni (Ed.), *Complex organizations: A sociological reader.* New York: Holt, Rinehart and Winston, 1961. Pp. 422–440.

Lineberry, R. L. Approaches to the study of community politics. In Charles M. Bonjean et al. (Eds.) *Community politics: A behavioral approach.* New York: 1971. Free Press, Pp. 16–25.

Marris, P., & Rein, M. *Dilemmas of social reform: Poverty and community action in the United States.* New York: Atherton Press, 1969.

Merton, R. K. *Social theory and social structure.* (Rev. and enlarged ed.) New York: The Free Press of Glencoe, 1957.

Poston, R. *Democracy is you.* New York: Harper & Row, 1953.

Rossi, P. H. Community social indicators. In Angus Campbell and Philip E. Converse, (Eds.) *The human meaning of social change.* New York: Russell Sage Foundation, 1972.

Rossi, P. H., & Williams, W. (Eds.) Evaluating social programs: *Theory, practice, and politics.* New York: Seminar Press, 1972.

Sanders, I. T. *Making good communities better.* Lexington, Ky.: University of Kentucky Press, 1953.

Suchman, E. A. *Evaluative research: Principles and practice in public service and social action programs.* New York: Russell Sage Foundation, 1967.

United States Chamber of Commerce. *Forward thrust: Guidelines for mobilizing total community resources.* Washington, D.C.: United States Chamber of Commerce, 1968.

Vanecko, J. J., et al. *Community organization efforts, political and institutional change, and the diffusion of change produced by community action programs.* Chicago: National Opinion Research Center, Report No. 122, 1970.

Voth, D. E. An evaluation of community development programs in Illinois. *Social Forces,* Vol 53 no. 4 1975.

Weiss, C. H. (Ed.) *Evaluating action programs: Readings in social action and education.* Boston: Allyn and Bacon, Inc., 1972.

Weiss, R. S., & Rein, M. The evaluation of broad-aim programs: Difficulties in experimental design and an alternative. In Carol H. Weiss, (Ed.), *Evaluating action programs: Readings in social action and education.* Boston: Allyn and Bacon, 1972. Pp. 236–249.

Wholey, J. S., et al. *Federal evaluation policy: Analyzing the effects of public programs.* Washington, D.C.: The Urban Institute, 1971.

Young, F. W., & Young, R. C. *Comparative studies of community growth.* Morgantown, W.Va.: West Virginia University Press, Rural Sociology Monograph Number Two, 1974.

PLANNED SOCIAL CHANGE AND THE NEGOTIATION OF REALITY: SOCIAL SCIENTISTS, POLICYMAKERS, AND PLANNERS*

Jerry A. Moles

Hesse (1970, p. 42) once wrote a short story in which God sent a flood that put an end to a bloody world war. The last European was struggling in the floodwaters when an ark appeared under the command of an aged patriarch named Noah, and the unfortunate man was hauled aboard. The crew of the ark was composed of persons from each ethnic group on earth. During the voyage each was called on to demonstrate his or her skill. Finally, the time for the European to perform came, and he informed his arkmates that he was skilled in the use of his intellect in solving the ". . . great problems on which the happiness of mankind depends."

*I have benefited from discussion with Paul W. Barkley, John W. Bennett, Sandra M. Gifford, R. J. Hildreth, L. M. Hartman, O. Norman Simpkins, and Donald M. Sorensen concerning some of the topics discussed in this chapter.

Noah was impressed.

> "The skill that brings happiness is certainly more important than any other. Just tell us what you know about the happiness of mankind. We shall all be grateful."

Up until then the European had been haughty and self-assured. Now he seemed at a loss.

> "It's not my fault," he said hesitantly, "but you still don't understand. I didn't say I knew the secret of happiness. I only said that my intellect is working on certain problems the solution of which would promote the happiness of mankind. Such work takes a long time, neither you nor I will live to see the end of it. The problems are knotty and many generations will continue to ponder them."
>
> The audience listened with mounting perplexity and distrust. What was the man saying? Even Noah averted his eyes and frowned.
>
> The Hindu smiled at the Chinese. When the others could think of nothing to say, the Chinese spoke up. "Dear brothers," he said most affably, "this white cousin is a joker. He is trying to tell us that his mind is working on something which our great-grandchildren's great-grandchildren may or may not live to see. I suggest that we applaud him as a joker. He says things that none of us can quite understand, but we all suspect that if we did fully understand them they would make us laugh and laugh and laugh."

Social scientists are, in ways, like the European. We are interested in human happiness; we speak of the quality of life, personal satisfaction, sense of security, and freedom from need. We use our intellect to assist others in reaching these objectives. We expect to spend much of our lives in the quest of ways to increase happiness while knowing that we may be unsuccessful. As a consequence, we run the risk of being called the joker. Our explanation, methods, and research techniques often do not provide adequate answers to many problems of pressing human concern. As Greer (1969) has noted,

> We have at best crude approximations of measurements for such variables as anomie ... sentiment, attitude, and the like. Yet we have theories that hypothesize invariant associations of these among themselves and with other aspects of behavior. We imagine the 'felicific calculus' with units of happiness, but in practice we use crude questions for a crude concept. (p. 129)

We run the risk of being called the joker when we ignore many of the limitations that exist in scientific inquiry and in the sharing of research results with policymakers, planners, and administrators who make decisions affecting our lives and the lives of others. I would like to discuss some of the limitations inherent in the scientific approach to the study of human behavior and suggest ways in which we can compensate for these shortcomings.

Science, and specifically the social sciences, constitutes one of the many subcultures in Western culture. For our purposes culture may be defined as human knowledge. This is similar to the idea proposed by Boulding (1956) in which he conceptualized culture as images of ourselves and our surroundings.

Human knowledge includes our percepts and concepts, our beliefs in which our percepts and concepts are organized into cause and effect relationships, our values that are used to organize our percepts and concepts into hierarchies of preference, and the ways in which we have organized our past experience of activities that were used to meet recurring needs into plans of action to meet these needs in the future. In short, culture consists of the information we use to decide what is, what can be, how we feel about things, what to do about things, and how to go about doing something about things (Goodenough, 1971).

The social science disciplines are composed of complex sets of interrelated concepts that describe and "explain" specific aspects of our social, cultural, and economic environment. Science, on the other hand, is a separate body of knowledge that is utilized to validate or justify statements derived from the interrelated concepts of a specific discipline in relationship with some empirical condition (Rudner, 1966). When used in combination, the knowledge from any discipline and the logic of justification from science constitute a set of powerful tools if they are applied with skill and insight but, like any other approach to understanding, they have their limitations. I would like to explore some of the ideas that have been developed concerning the nature of knowledge and relate them to social science inquiry and the uses of social science in the solution of human problems.

Knowledge is reality. What we know, our percepts and concepts, our beliefs, our values, our skills, our awareness of ourselves and others, and our awareness of our environment constitute our reality. What we know is what we are. I know what I am by knowing my relationships with all other persons and things, past and present. In this sense knowledge is time binding; it permits me to use my memory of past experiences in interpreting the present and in anticipating the future. I know there are many things I do not know; this, too, is a part of my reality. Even the things I do not know are interpreted on the basis of the things that I do know. I know there are other realities. I know that I will learn about the realities of other people, but I can only interpret them on the basis of my reality, on the basis of my knowledge, because that is all that I have. I cannot share your experience, but we can experience things at the same time and place. You can experience me and I can experience you. I can tell you about my experiences, but my telling you of my experiences does not allow you to experience them. You can only interpret my experiences on the basis of your own experiences. As both Hume and Russell have shown, knowledge is ultimately derived from individual human experience.

Knowledge is "truth." While we may only be sure of our own death, (something we often tend to ignore), there are other things that we accept as true. We ignore the philosophical complexities, receive information from our interactions with the environment, and place our faith in this information. Of course, we know things that are false from our point of view, but knowing that they are false is for us a "truth." We may erroneously accept a falsehood as being true but, until we discover that it is false, it remains true for us. In this sense some philosophers claim there is no false information, there is just information.

Knowledge is an adaptative "tool" and is more highly developed by *Homo sapiens* than by any other species. It is used to guide our behavior and to interpret the behavior of others. Our ways of knowing permit social intercourse and communication. We use information to reduce the complexity of the environment. We do this through the creation of abstract categories or equivalance classes. We simply do not have the requisite neurological circuitry to isolate and classify every discernible entity in our surroundings. For example, it has been estimated that we receive 10,000 bits of information per millisecond through our visual apparatus. As a result, we have the ability to detect from 7,500,000 to 10,000,000 distinct colors (Optical Society of America, 1953). It would be impossible to remember that many colors, nor would it be useful to do so. Instead, we reduce the complexity of visual inputs by organizing the universe of color into equivalance classes. Colors that seem to be similar are combined into classes and are separated from other groups of colors that seem to be different. We organize other aspects of our environment in much the same manner. The things we isolate and categorize are usually important to our lives in some way and are things about which we must make decisions (Brown, 1965, pp. 332–335).

We further simplify the environment by organizing categories into more complex structures. Classes of entities are organized into hierarchies of abstraction that range from the specific to the general. The degree of abstraction is determined by the level of specifity required to identify things about which we must decide in the course of our lives. For example, a Hanunoo rice farmer in the Philippines can classify more than 80 discrete kinds of rice (Conklin, 1957). Different kinds of rice are planted at different times, are cultivated in different ways, and vary according to taste and texture. The farmer makes decisions concerning his activities based in part on his classification of types of rice. For a majority of persons in North America, fewer than 10 classes of rice constitute an adequate set of categories for the decisions we must make. In this instance, North Americans tend to be more general in their classification than Hanunoo farmers. The Hanunoo can be just as abstract when considering all rice as constituting a single category, but he can also be more specific when breaking this single class into more than 80 types.

In the process of reducing the complexity of the environment, we select a limited number of indicators that enable us to anticipate the future consequence of our actions and the actions of others. We are always in the process of attempting to create and maintain a predictable world. We fear the unpredictable, as we fear chaos, and we continually create new knowledge to interpret and assign meaning to the present and to anticipate the future (Garfinkle, 1972; Goodenough, 1971; Mehan & Wood, 1975). Novak (1971), in his discussion of knowledge as culture, noted,

> Experience rushes in upon us in such floods that we must break it down, select from it, abstract, shape and relate. . . . A culture is constituted by the meaning it imposes on human experience . . . even the most solid and powerful social insti-

tutions, though they may imprison us, improverish us, or kill us, are fundamentally mythical structures designed to hold chaos and formlessness at bay . . . culture begins and ends in the void. (p. 29)

Knowledge is also adaptive in that new knowledge is created in the attempt to solve problems. We apply our energies to problems and develop new ways of viewing certain aspects of the environment. As a result, increased specialization is possible. As Simpkins (1977) has noted, there is an increase of information with the development of occupational specialization. In the past, when farmers served as their own blacksmiths, veterinarians, bankers, and the like, there was a limit to the amount of knowledge that could be developed and brought to bear on any single problem. As people left farming and specialized in these areas, new knowledge was created and important break-throughs occurred. A part of the creation of new knowledge includes the development of ways in which to search for knowledge. Scientific methodology has been one result of the search for new information.

Knowledge tends to be created at a conservative rate. Wallace (1961) points out that two major problems must be solved by all people: we must replicate uniformity and organize diversity. We replicate uniformity in order to make our behavior intelligible to others and to interpret their behavior, to use the skills and knowledge that have proven successful in the past to meet the needs of the present, and to reduce the need to learn continually *de novo* from new experiences or, said another way, to reduce the high cost of new information. We organize diversity so that we can interpret new situations, know how to handle new conditions, and learn from our mistakes. Consequently, we try to limit the rate of change in knowledge to a level that we can control. It is often to our advantage to maintain the *status quo* if we are in a satisfactory position. In some cases, when we are not in a satisfactory position, we do not attempt to change because the circumstances in which we exist are at least predictable, if not comfortable. We are often amazed in development programs when farmers refuse to adopt a new crop that we believe would be advantageous. If they have had no experience with the new crop and cannot anticipate their return, they may reject our offer. The cost of the new information is too high in that they must risk their livelihood to determine the yield of the new alternative.

Knowledge systems seem to be conservative in another way. Levi-Strauss (1973) has pointed out in his study of mythology that knowledge systems tend to be circular and closed. It is possible to start at any point in a set of myths that describes and explains some phenomena and eventually work back to the starting point. Any set of knowledge including science or any discipline can be viewed as a type of mythology in that it is a set of interrelated abstractions used to account for certain kinds of phenomena and to direct specific activities. Generally, each of us accepts our view of the world as adequate at the moment for describing and explaining our world. The things that we cannot describe and explain are often labeled unimportant and not worthy of the efforts required to learn about them. If circumstances were otherwise, we would make the effort. Although it is true that we continually search for new information in attempts to solve problems and learn from experience and that there is always a degree of novelty in behavior, our learning is always based on previously accumulated knowledge. Furthermore, we often ignore information that cannot be related to what we presently know because we have not learned to identify it; consequently, it falls outside of our range of awareness. We do not break the circle of understanding but, instead, continously expand it while maintaining the integrity of its boundaries. We are victims of our past and cannot disassociate ourselves from our experience. In science we close the circle by calling what we are unable to account for "the unknown" and, in this manner, we control the mysteries of the universe. In a sense the concept of the unknown is a category related to the environment, even though it is a residual one. We often say that the purpose of science is to make the unknown known and take comfort in this view; however, the unknown we speak of is delimited by present knowledge and the realm of discourse selected. In statistics, we close the explanatory circle by calling unexplained variance a measurement error, but it is difficult to explain why it is an error or how to correct such an error. As noted earlier, we seem to have a special abhorrence of mystery and the unknown, we do not like to know and, as a consequence, are very inventive in our attempts to close our conceptual circles. By keeping these circles closed, however, we reject potentially useful information.

Knowledge and thereby reality and "truth" are human creations. Knowledge is derived from experience and is created as we attempt to solve problems. Even though we have learned concepts that were developed in the distant past, they are only meaningful when applied to the present in which they are learned and related to information gained from experience. Furthermore, as Wagner (1975) has suggested, when existing categories are applied, things in the present are made equivalent to things in the past; therefore this act of categorization is creative. After all, we have never been in this present before, nor will we return. When new categories are created to interpret the environment, things that have never existed are invented. When we conceive of things that have never existed and make them occur, we have created reality. In science we create the reality that we report on. The reality we "discover" is partly determined by the conceptual approach selected and the operational definitions or measurement techniques created to represent theoretical concepts and partly by the phenomena selected for study. For example, in quantum physics it is possible to view light either as waves or as particles, depending on the measurement technique used and the research question at hand. We create variability by placing discrete entities into a single category and looking at two or more of them using one of more additional categories as variables.

We create reality each time we select among alternatives. Regrettably, we have only one life to live in this plane of existence, and the present is the eternity in which we all must live. When we select one television program over another or over mowing the lawn, we have created our reality. Moreover, in the social sciences we create additional realities to "explain" the realities we select and create. Economic theory states that we select among alternatives in a "rational" manner and that the things selected have more "value" than the things not selected. We assume that we can place a value on the alternative selected and imply that we can place a lower value on alternatives not selected. The concept of opportunity cost was created to "explain" the selective creation of reality. Furthermore, the concept closes a rather obvious conceptual circle.

Part of our reality is created privately, and we do not attempt to share it with others. Other aspects of reality are negotiated with others and are determined through consensus or at least through an agreement not to disagree anymore. We will never know the perceptions and conceptions of another person. If I could see through your eyes, what I normally see as white might appear to be green. If you could see through my eyes, what you see as white might appear to be purple. Nonetheless, we have both agreed to call the green and the purple white, so we will concur that your shirt is white. Such Consensus is usually referred to as intersubjective agreement. What we call the "objective" approach in science is based on a number of negotiations that have transpired over the years in conversations, journals, and books. We have accepted certain standards for scientific endeavors or have agreed that further discussion is not productive. What we call "objectivity" in scientific inquiry is based on a set of intersubjective agreements.

Some people have greater skill in negotiating reality and "truth"; they may have greater power, or they may have considerable influence and consequently have a strong hand in the determination of reality based on inter-subjective agreement. Nietzsche (1955) once wrote,

> . . . *the real philosophers are commanders and legislators.* They say, "It *shall* be thus!" They determine the "whither" and the "to what end" of mankind—having the preliminary work of all workers in philosophy, the overpower of the past, at their disposal. But they grope with creative hands toward the future—everything that is and was becomes their means, their instrument, their hammer. Their "knowing" is *creating*. (p. 54)

I would add that many others including people in business, scientists, teachers, and government administrators play similar roles.

We are often unaware of our creation and negotiation of "truth" and reality. We accept what we have learned and use it creatively without question. We accept social order, including interpersonal interaction and economic transaction as "natural." Yet as Berger and Luckmann (1966) have pointed out,

> Social order is not part of the "nature of things," and it cannot be derived from the "laws of nature." Social order exists *only* as a product of human activity. . . . Both in its genesis . . . and its existence in any instant of time (social order exists only insofar as human activity continues to produce it) it is a human product. (p. 52)

We now return to an issue raised earlier, the limitations of science in the study of human behavior and in communicating research results with other people. We must first focus our attention on the scientific study of behavior. Any social science approach is used like all other knowledge systems to reduce the complexity of the environment. Human behavior is a continuous stream that occurs day after day, and we cannot hope to deal with all of its variety and richness. As a result, we only deal with limited aspects of human activity. When specific areas of inquiry are selected, it becomes obvious that an increased number of categories are required to account for the variability encountered. After all, science advances with increased specification. As specification increases, it becomes more difficult for any researcher to remain aware of much of the behavior of the people under study. Therefore, any research report that meets contemporary scientific standards usually tells us very little about a wide range of activities that may influence the specific behavior under investigation. For example, Schultz (1968) noted that some growth models in economics have treated institutions as givens, or as a part of the "state of nature," while others have treated institutions as independent of economic change. Economists have studied the management of capital, labor, and technology on farms while ignoring the social structure that supports agriculture. Anthropologists have studied the social structure of rural communities while ignoring the economic aspects. It is clear, however, that we cannot account for economic behavior by the study of social structure alone. Even if economists, anthropologists, sociologists, and the like worked together, we would never be able to describe and explain adequately the behavior of farmers or anyone else. We view brief instances of their lives, but they live their lives on a full-time basis. Although one objective of science is to generalize, increased specification reduces the ability to do so because of our limited capacity to control information. Also, the number of specifications are limitless; they are created by scientists and are limited only by the creativity of their minds. We are caught in a double-bind; to have confidence in our results we must increase specifications but, in the process, we lose sight of the subject of inquiry, people living in a particular time and place.

Social scientists have tended to follow the scientific paradigms created by the physical scientists. Becker (1968, p. 387) noted that this narrow positivist approach, which seeks to analyze separate and distinct aspects of behavior, was bound to fail. Because of the limited realm of inquiry in physics and the degree of control a physicist can exert over the phenomena, the positivistic approach is plausible; however, as Ritchie (1958, p. 186) has noted, the approach has encountered serious difficulties in biology. Given the complexity in human behavior, these difficulties are compounded in social inquiry. Boulding (1968, p. 9) commented that at the level of understanding human behavior ". . . it may be doubted whether we have as yet even the rudiments of theoretical systems." Wittgenstein (1922, p. 6.52) may have been correct, at least for the foreseeable future, when he suggested, ". . . that even after all possible scientific questions have been answered, our problems of existence have not even been touched upon."

Despite the limitations in science, we remain in the business of the creation of social "fact." It can be argued that social science works, and I agree. We create "truths" in which we can have a degree of faith. Social science works best, however, when the "truths" discovered are passed to nonscientists who have the power to construct social realities. Let me explain. We create approaches based on theory, method, and the phenomena studied. As would be expected, a close congruency is created between disciplines and the environment. In recent history, as the practitioners of the disciplines, especially the economists, became more proficient, the information created was used in government and business. What began as academic discourse became a working culture used to guide decisions in important sectors of society, thereby increasing the congruency between scientific approaches and the social and economic environment. What had at one point been a conceptual formulation became transformed with the aid of political and economic power into social "fact." Consequently, the descriptive and explanatory powers of social science increased. The view that science works best when the categories created become part of the knowledge used by persons in positions of power is supported by experiences in developing nations. Our descriptive and explanatory growth models do not work as well in the Third World. Social scientists have not had the same opportunity to participate in the creation of social "reality" in these areas as they have had in the more developed nations.

We now turn our attention to some of the limitations present in communicating results with policymakers, planners, and so on. All social scientists specialize in one narrow aspect of behavior, and the advice we give is based on a narrow range of data. Planners, policymakers, developers, and the like, however, demand that we generalize; they want to create programs for all farmers and all workers, and they expect us to provide valid information concerning a broad population. They may have had very different experiences than scientists have had, may have created different realities, and may be unaware of the fragile base of social science. Furthermore, they want information immediately so that they can get on with the job. Consequently, we have little time to negotiate a reality concerning the limitations of what we know and its relationship to the program envisioned. There is a jump in levels of abstration from the specific data developed by scientists to the generalities used by planners and the relationship between the specific, and the general is often tenuous. Furthermore, planners and policymakers may add to the information presented by the scientists in ways that suggest that the scientists produced the additional material. Although there may be no information other than what the social scientists may present, planners and policymakers often feel free to add material based on little more than personal conviction, reinterpret the findings, and draw new conclusions that may or may not be warranted without additional empirical investigation. The scientists have no control over such actions. The "truth" we create continues to be used and reinterpreted many times. Policymakers pass the information along to program administrators who, in turn, pass it along to change agents or field staffs who, in turn, pass it along to the population for whom the program was developed. At each step, the information is reinterpreted based on the experiences of specific individuals and the social environment in which they exist. There is a kind of "situational logic" in operation; each decisionmaker decides that if a particular policy or program is to become operational, it must be made congruent with his or her own view of the world. What started as specific information based on scientific inquiry becomes a social reality; in some cases, it is difficult for the scientist who created the information to recognize the final results of his or her handicraft.

Scientists are often unaware of their blind spots when they give advice to policymakers. As Barkley (1975) has noted,

> Too often, the economist has been asked a quick and pragmatic question and has responded with a quick and pragmatic answer. How do you eliminate poverty? By giving people more money. . . . How do you improve incomes in agriculture? By supporting the price of grains. These questions have been given quick and explicit answers but those providing answers have not taken time to learn of possible side effects the answers might bring. (p. 4)

The same is true in other disciplines. Frequently scientists are not aware or ignore the limits to their knowledge. As noted earlier, all knowledge systems tend to be circular and closed, and we tend to ignore other viewpoints. Space limitations prevent a discussion of the topic, but it should be mentioned that the information we create may be more useful to one group than to another and can possibly give advantages to some at the expense of others. When we assume that knowledge is adaptive, we should always consider to whom it is adaptive.

Knowledge produced through scientific inquiry has another limitation when used in program development. Our descriptions and explanations are based on a narrow range of information, and when we attempt to generalize to other circumstances, we should always mention that our statements hold *ceteris paribus,* "all other things being equal." When we deal with responses to known phenomena or similar conditions, we have some idea of the unknown variables implicit in *ceteris paribus.* On the other hand, when we are asked what the impact of some program that has never been tried will be, we have little information on which to base a prediction. Science deserts us at this point, as does every other knowledge system. It is not possible to predict what we do not know from past experience. Prediction is always based on the past plus the hope that we are correct in the future. Most of us have not been trained as program planners, but as scientists, and our knowledge of the operations of programs may be limited. It is wise at times to say that we do not know.

Where does all of this leave us? I think that we must accept the limitations of the scientific approach to the study of human behavior and attempt to make policymakers and planners aware of these limitations. We should remain mindful of the role we have had in the past in the creation of social reality and in this light accept the responsibility for the consequence of our statements. Given the limitations of science, I believe we should support less centralized planning and permit local people to keep their resources at home, set their own priorities, and assume responsibilities for their lives insofar as possible. Schumacher (1973, p. 250) notes that the administrators in any large organization are in a difficult position. They assume the responsibility for everything that happens without having the information or the time available to make adequate decisions. As organizations become larger and larger, people lose local control over their communities and their lives. Attempts to create policies and programs that are applicable to an entire nation or state often result in policies and programs that are not appropriate in any particular set of circumstances. Yet persons in power remain in their current positions by passing wealth through their hands for redistribution in return for various types of political and economic resources. The disclaimer is often issued that planners and policymakers cannot do a more satisfactory job because they do not have adequate information or the time to acquire such information. Sadly, such protests are often valid because the structural alignments within large organizations preclude the opportunity to deal with specific local problems. Nonetheless, persons in positions of power are seldom willing to pass along the control they possess to local level public and economic organizations, the very level at which the information and time required to make decisions relative to specific conditions could be made available. Furthermore, if planning was conducted at the local level, the people for whom the plans were being made would have access to the planners, which would help to insure the appropriateness of any suggested program. Too frequently people who have power criticize the general public for not being more responsible for their lives and fail to see the irony in the situation when they refuse to make any effort to release the resources that would make such responsibility possible. Of course, I realize that every decision cannot be made on a local level. We do live in a complex and interrelated world, and some degree of central planning is necessary. An important task for the future is to determine the levels at which programs can be most effectively carried out and the information that will be required to assist in the process.

Despite the limitations inherent in the use of scientific methods in social inquiry, I believe that it remains the single best way to find out what is going on in the world. We must be very careful to determine what kinds of questions can and cannot be answered through the use of scientific procedures. There are areas in which we can work with some effectiveness. First, we can evaluate programs and study the creation of social reality by policymakers and planners. Do programs really produce the consequences they were intended to produce? What are the unintended side effects of programs? Who benefits and who is disadvantaged by policy decisions? We have skills that can be put to use in answering these and similar questions at local, regional, and national levels. We may never be able to answer the question of what will work, but we can determine if things are not working as intended. Second, social scientists can monitor other social processes that may or may not be directly related to policy decisions but that may pose a threat to one or more segments of the society. Environmental degradation, social costs of technology, inequality of opportunity, health care—the list is endless, and these things require constant scrutiny. John W. Bennett, the eminent American anthropologist, once suggested to me that the social sciences would be well served if more of us behaved as investigative reporters. I believe that the monitoring process I have suggested is related to such an investigative task. Third, I believe that social scientists can work effectively in communities to determine the desires and needs of specific populations and to provide the information necessary for planning at the local level. Too frequently information is collected at the local level and presented to state and national officials without any input from community members for whom the plans are being made. People receive sewage treatment plants when they would have preferred loans for home improvement, road repair when a medical clinic would have been more useful, and new road signs announcing the name of the community when street lights would have been more appreciated.

In order to evaluate programs and monitor social processes, we must work toward more inclusive paradigms or approaches such as the one proposed by Simpkins (1977) based on the concept of scale. A great deal of effort needs to be directed toward the development of a more unified theory of human behavior in which the diverse aspects of behavior studied by the various disciplines can be organized in a way that can be related to specific populations. It may be that such a unified approach is impossible. We are never going to be able to deal with human creativity and the diversity of behavior that it produces, but such a search will be useful if it only reminds us of our limitations from time to time. Such reminders are needed because, as noted earlier, all systems of knowledge tend toward circularity and closure.

Finally, even if we only evaluate programs and monitor social processes, we will continue to create social "facts" and be involved in the construction of social reality. When we embark on any research endeavor, we must remain aware of the possible consequence of our actions. We make difficult decisions, and there are no clear guidelines to follow. Becker (1968) has suggested that we give some thought to the ethical and moral issues involved in social inquiry. We claim that we are not biased but, on closer inspection, the claim that there is an absence of bias is, in fact, a bias. I believe that such a claim is an attempt to avoid the responsibility for our findings and statements. There are no value free or neutral paradigms. We cannot cling to our present approaches by simply claiming that they constitute the best viewpoint currently available. Although they may offer us some security and provide a consistent framework for exploring the world, they are used at some cost to ourselves and to the people whose lives are changed because of the realities we have helped create. We must become involved in determining the costs of our descriptions and explanations. As we become more aware of our limitations and our role in the creation of social reality, I believe that moral and ethical questions will weigh more heavily on us.

I have one last thought to share. Scientific disciplines are limited because they are systems of human knowledge. On the other hand, since we create them, scientific disciplines are unlimited; they can be so much more than what they are.

BIBLIOGRAPHY AND REFERENCES

Barkely, P. W. Economics and small units: An arena of intellectual poverty. Paper presented at the Mathematical Social Science Board Conference on Standardization and Measurement. Coloma, California, May 1975. p. 4

Becker, E. *The structure of evil.* New York: The Free Press, 1968.

Berger, P. L., & Luckmann, T. *The social construction of reality.* Garden City, N.Y.: Doubleday, 1966.

Boulding, K. E. General systems theory—The skeleton of science. In Walter Buckley (Ed.), *Modern systems research for the behavioral scientist.* Chicago: Aldine, 1968, pp. 3–10.

Boulding, K. E. *The image.* Ann Arbor, Mich.: University of Michigan Press, 1956.

Brown, R. *Social psychology.* New York: The Free Press, 1965.

Conklin, H. C. *Hanunoo agriculture.* Rome: FAO, United Nations, 1957.

Garfinkel, H. Remarks on ethnomethodology. In John J. Gumperz and Dell Hymes, (Eds.), *Directions in sociolinguistics.* New York: Holt, Rinehart & Winston, 1972, pp. 310–324.

Goodenough, W. H. *Culture, language and society.* McCaleb Module in Anthropology. New York: Addison-Wesley, 1971.

Greer, S. *The logic of social inquiry.* Chicago: Aldine, 1969.

Hesse, H. *If the war goes on.* New York: Bantam Books, 1970.

Hume, D. *An inquiry concerning human understanding.* Indianapolis: Bobbs-Merrill, 1955.

Levi-Strauss, C. *From honey to ashes.* New York: Harper & Row, 1973.

Mehan, H., & Wood, H. *The reality of ethnomethodology.* New York: John Wiley, 1975.

Nietzche, F. *Beyond good and evil.* New York: Macmillan, 1973.

Novak, M. *The experience of nothingness.* New York: Harper & Row, 1971.

Optical Society of America, Committee on Colorimetry. *The science of color.* New York: Crowell, 1953.

Ritchie, A. D. *Studies in the history and methods of science.* Edinburgh: The University Press, 1958.

Rudner, R. S. *Philosophy of social science.* Englewood Cliffs,: N.J. Prentice-Hall, 1966.

Russell, B. *The problems of philosophy.* London: Home University Library, 1912.

Schultz, T. W. The institutions and the rising economic value of man. *Am. J. Ag. Econ.,* 1968, **50,** 1113–1122.

Schumacher, E. F. *Small is beautiful: Economics as if people mattered.* London: Blond and Briggs, 1973.

Simpkins, O. N. A "scale" approach to community development. Paper presented at the American Agricultural Economics Association Meetings, San Diego, California, August 1977.

Wagner, R. *The invention of culture.* Englewood Cliffs, N.J.: Prentice-Hall, 1975.

Wallace, A. F. C. *Culture and personality.* New York: Random House, 1961.

Wittgenstein, L. *Tractatus logico-philosophicus.* London: Routledge and Kegan, 1922.

Chapter 10

THE COMMUNITY DEVELOPMENT SPECIALIST'S ROLE IN COMMUNITY RESEARCH: CREATING TRUST AND MANAGING POWER*

James G. Kelly

The emergence of community development as a field with multiple origins, ranging from social action to social planning, does not have clarity. Economists, sociologists, and anthropologists are not certain that the community development specialist's work differs from that of the social worker, the applied economist, or other professions. Community-based research, however, provides a unique opportunity to extend the traditional discipline values for reflection, theorizing, and empirical analysis to the needed area of analysis of social issues.

Vallance (1972, p. 108) has outlined seven steps for community research: clarifying awareness of problems, describing problems in detail, formulating problem-solving approaches, identifying community resources needed for solutions, specifying additional resources needed and

*Paper presented at the symposium "Knowledge and Technology in Community Psychology" at the 82nd Annual Meeting of the American Psychological Association, New Orleans, Louisiana, September 1, 1974.

available in the community, evaluating and implementing solutions, and encouraging community members to extend and use the research process. These steps suggest new knowledge for the field of community development with potential benefits for citizens. Communities may benefit from a professional who knows how to be both scientific and useful; there is certainly ample opportunity to relate disciplined thinking to topics of public concern. The tasks of doing community research and developing a theory of the research process provide a source of special identity for the development specialist.

There are three features in the research process that seem important. One is the relationship between the researcher and the community; what roles will the development specialist adopt in the community—advocate, participant observer, or dispassionate investigator? The second issue is the choice of research methods for the particular occasion; are the preferred methods a journalistic account of community events, a systematic, observational study, or a controlled study with quasiexperimental design? These have been discussed in earlier chapters. The third issue is the process for evaluating research experiences so that the education and training of (future) community development specialists can be helped; how will understanding community power structures and resistance to change, or the relationship of research findings to public policy, be available as topics for the education of community developers? These three features can get us started toward a conception of community research as a process. If the community developer takes more advantage of opportunities for community-based research, a theory of community research as a process will be needed. To start, I offer the premise that community research involves incremental stages, over time, that vary from community to community.

How can the development specialist be true to the scientific and ethical traditions of the social sciences *and* be authentic to the needs for knowledge in different communities? How will the specialist adapt to these potentially conflicting demands and manage the tension generated by these two values: reflection and utility? How will the community developer manage this tension in order to develop the quality of the development specialist's work and the viability of community development as a field of work?

I argue that the community development specialist cannot revere one method but, instead, must value multiple modes of inquiry and must creatively manage the tension between basic inquiry and utility. The role of the community developer cannot be captivated by scientificism or elitism. The adaptive requirements are for research to be an improvised process that involves an active and reciprocal relationship with citizens. Consequently, the community developer cannot impose the varied and multiple methods of choice upon a community. The influences and respect derived from the specialist's choice of methods in the laboratory too often can be unrelated to citizens' needs. Kelman (1972), in a very insightful challenge to the laboratory research ethic, has advocated a frame of reference for all community research as participatory research, designed to involve persons as active participants in a joint effort with the investigator. This orientation is particularly appropriate for the research process related to community psychology, and it demands that more specific attention be given to defining the roles of citizens and researchers in the research enterprise under different community conditions. Certainly not all conditions are under our control or are comfortable.

In a discussion of urban children's views on research, Cottle (1974) included the perceptions of some parents. A very apt quotation, referring to a mother's perception of scientists, is applicable to the community researcher and goes like this.

> "Rich folks is what they are, no different from all the rest. Sitting over there . . . playing with this and playing with that. Making up problems where problems don't really exist. Making things complicated when really what we need done is so simple a child could understand." Her tone was bitter. "Every day I read in the papers about the money they get to do all those experiments with whatever you call what they do over there. And not only over there at your place, but all across this land. In all the colleges! What I want to know is what good are they doing for this country?" (p. 36)

The process of choosing topics for investigation and the methods of inquiry require an incubation period that includes ample time for the mutual accommodation of the specialist and the community. This time period usually exceeds the time alloted for the design of laboratory research and the technical preparation of data. The process of knowing the community, of understanding the premises that citizens have about "outsiders," "intellectuals" and "professors," "professionals," and "liberals" is a process that varies from place to place, but it is a process that the development specialist endures and learns from. This process of defining entry into the community and working conditions for community research can be called "learning to create trust." Trust exists when persons expect that the community developer means and does what he or she says. It not only refers to whether citizens can predict the behavior of the community developer, but whether the community developer will be useful and valued no matter what the research finally reports.

John Coelho organized an SPSSI-sponsored symposium at the American Psychological Association in 1971. One of the participants, Torres (1973), summarized her comments by asserting that applied social science research did present some new issues.

But as social scientists turn to work oriented toward current social problems, and with groups already defining the social scientist as one of those problems, whole sets of new issues, relationships, and responsibilities arise which we are only beginning to identify and face. It will take considerable sensitivity and ingenuity to develop the attitudes and habits necessary to work out appropriate and fruitful relations with the many parties now involved. We must begin with the recognition that an orientation toward the needs of those one studies need not preclude a disciplined search for knowledge and an understanding that while the social scientist and those he studies do not, and cannot, have the same objectives, they can and must have complementary ones. (p. 216)

One of the themes that evolved at the symposium was the need for action research to be more conscious of the client. Kahn (1973), a discussant at the same symposium, said what we have often known but not spoken.

The point seems obvious enough, but it has been characteristically ignored by social scientists. They have too often insisted on groping for explanations and inventing social remedies or policies while the client waited. The result was that clients often waited beyond the point where research could be helpful or, since remedy invention is always difficult, they were offered the cure to which the scientist was addicted rather than something adapted to their special needs. (p. 245)

But awareness of community needs is not enough. Community-based research requires a shift in values by the research investigator. Caplan and Nelson (1973) sharply stated the issue in taking the applied researcher to task and in asking for a value shift in research.

It is the good will and approval of our colleagues in the scientific community, not that of the target population members affected by our work, that get us ahead. A social scientist's findings may provide or influence the underlying

assumptions on which "corrective" programs affecting
thousands or perhaps millions of persons will be predicated.
It is ironic, then, that his career gains will depend more on
his contribution to the advancement of his discipline from
studying applied problems than on the success or failure of
those programs. (p. 205)

As the community developer makes the value shift and
pays increasing attention to the community demands of
research, there is a need to consider the variables that affect
the research process within community settings. This
sometimes slow and gradual process of defining the trust
relationship between the community and the specialist is
also affected by the community developer's efforts to
understand the process of power, the control of resources.
If the results of community research have impact for the
community, a change in a public policy is expected to shift
the control of resources in order to create a new community service, alter a public policy so that new persons receive a service, or encourage more or different citizens to
influence policymaking. Knowing much more about processes of power, its sources, and its management is necessary if community research is to be scientific and useful.

The challenge to the community developer is not only
to be technically competent, but to create a working knowledge of the community as well. Trust and power are
proposed as two processes for helping the community developer to conduct research that will be constructive to the
community. What is important is to specify how different
levels of trust and power affect the varied roles that the
community development specialist takes in the research
process.

The community developer, I argue, needs a conception of the research enterprise that puts aside previous
assumptions about inquiry. The community developer will
need to adopt new premises such as: (1) all knowledge is

not good; (2) some knowledge may be useful, but only to certain people; (3) high-quality data can be interpreted for bad purposes; (4) low-quality data can be a catalyst for justice; and (5) the communication of "good" data can have negative outcomes. The freedom that a community developer is given to do research in a community requires new ethics when the research process intrudes into ongoing community events and touches pockets of vested interest.

The research roles for the community developer involve many risks. There are risks when presenting oneself as a scientist with complete neutrality, as an observer with no commitment to report what is becoming known, or as a partisan who shares the interests of some community. Performing roles such as these without a rationale for long-term effects costs time, wastes the resources of the researcher, and limits opportunities for the community to develop new resources. Besides, a community will have doubts about any scientist who represents neutrality on public issues. Citizens know from their life experiences that no person has a right to observe without a return, and they have learned that an outsider with common sense will not advocate partisanship for a cause without an initial assessment of possibilities for success. A schema derived from the axiom that research is a process, a process where knowledge is designed to influence policy, is presented (Table 10–1). The premise is that social values, including values for research, vary in different communities, and that community conditions and options for research roles are interrelated. The premise is ecological.

In this schema the variables are support, trust, and power (see Table 10–1). It is hypothesized that varying combinations of support, trust, and power will affect the adaptive requirements of research roles. The type of community context (supportive versus nonsupportive), the community level of trust (high or low) for the research process, and the level of power (high or low) the commu-

Table 10–1 Schemata for the Research Roles of the Community Psychologist and Their Impact on Community Development Under Two Conditions of Support, Trust, and Power

		Supportive context (long tenure for research process)	*Nonsupportive context* (short tenure for research process)
High trust (high expectations for good research by community)	*High power* (high influence option offered research)	Low potential for research as community development	High potential for community analysis
	Low power (low influence option offered research)	High potential for revising research styles	High potential for research improvisation
Low trust (low expectations for good research by community)	*High power* (high influence option offered research)	High potential for research as community development	High potential for community criticism
	Low power (low influence option offered research)	Low potential for community based research	Low potential except for rehearsal for research in a new community

nity is attributing to the research investigator make up the initial framework. These variables of community support, trust, and perceived power suggest the varied roles in which research is performed and the impact of the research experience on the community developer. The interplay between the supportive level of the community, attributed trust, and attributed power for the community developer will generate adaptive roles for carrying out the research work. *Community support* assumes a moderate and consistent political, economic, and social support for the performance of community research. *Attributed trust* is defined as expectations by a cross section of citizens that the research process will lead to good effects. The variable of *attributed power* affirms that a cross section of citizens are giving the community researcher the option to influence the community. These three variables are viewed as continual, but are dichotomized for clarity and simplicity.

THE SUPPORTIVE CONTEXT WHERE TRUST AND POWER ARE HIGH: THE COMMUNITY PSYCHOLOGIST IS ALIVE AND WELL IN THE LAND OF OZ

This rare and perhaps illusory condition where all resources and influences are present and active on the researcher's behalf is an idyllic view of what community research can be like. There is freedom to do research that is self-designed; the research process begins from the researcher's opinions of what to study.

This condition is most supportive for the role of experimental research to help social progress. Campbell's (1969) concept of experimental research as a force in social reform can be most easily accommodated under conditions where support, trust, and power are present. Campbell's charge goes as follows.

> What is . . . essential is that the social scientist research advisor understand the political realities of the situation, and that he aid by helping create a public demand for hard headed evaluation, by contributing to those political inventions that reduce the liability of honest evaluation, and by educating future administrators to the problems and possibilities. (p. 409)

The role of the investigator as advisor, where there is an opportunity to carry out empirical work to test out alternative solutions to problems with the sense that data will be used in policymaking, is a very desirable setting for playing out research work without interference. It is a condition to be worked for, but I do not think the condition will appear very often in a local community. In the local community, the specialist, as an outsider, will need time to create support, trust, and power. Such freedom can be earned, but only over a period of time. Even when the three conditions are present, the apparent freedom has a cost. As the good fit between the expectations of the community developer and the community is expressed, few of the research tasks are expected to require the specialist to examine the precise benefits of the research for the total community. Extra spunk and integrity may be needed to encourage the community developer to ask persons to say aloud that the research may be misguided and to state how the research can be improved. The challenge for research under this environmental condition is to help the environmental conditions of support, trust, and power serve as a new force to stimulate the various leaderships within the community to worry more seriously about local conditions. The challenge of this environmental condition is for community research to be a "foil against complacency." While the adaptive requirements of this situation are expected to involve minimum strain and conflict, the opportunity is present for the research process to use the support, trust, and power as a means of identifying how unmet needs can be met by more, if not all, persons who live there. The community developer can generate further trust and esteem for his or her work, however, if the research is designed to detect social issues that have been reported and discussed as community issues. If the community developer assumes the role of competent investigator, he or she has an opportunity to serve as a role model of how research is accountable when solving social issues.

This desirable yet rare condition of Oz has an impact on the choice of research roles to be performed. It is expected that the community developer under these conditions will select a favorite technique, a concept, or a theoretical perspective and will stay with it. There will, perhaps, be few external demands for experimentation, and the research role can easily fit the perspective and traditions of the specialist's previous training. One of the primary shortcomings of this particular condition is not only that research will be noncontroversial, but that this pleasantly congruent condition between the environment and the investigator reduces the need to transmit knowledge for the future training of community developers. The prospects for developing future programs of research training are dim, and few new experiences are expected to be passed on to the new generation. Comfort *is* unchallenging.

THE SUPPORTIVE CONTEXT WHERE TRUST IS HIGH, YET POWER IS LOW: THE COMMUNITY DEVELOPER AS HORATIO ALGER

Under this condition the community developer is asked to prove his or her worth. The community developer, however, in this situation, knows that if he or she performs, he or she will be able to have influence. This condition can affect the specialist's choice of topics to study, the choice of variables for research, and the extra attention to be given to insure that research results are communicated to the right people. The effect of this environmental condition is expected to be that the performance of research will be skewed toward actions that help the researcher to achieve full membership in the community. Research roles and research work are likely to be adopted that stimulate the choice of topics and the selection of variables that can be carried out with ease and can have a rapid cycle from idea to result. Efficiency, simplicity, and responsiveness are the norm for the research process under this condition.

The learning derived from this condition is higher than in the previous condition. This environmental condition can help the investigator to learn the skills that are involved when quickly developing a research design that leads to clear results, the quick study that teases truth. The environmental condition can stimulate research that helps the community to become more efficient and self-conscious of its resources. The challenge for the community developer working under this condition is to rise above the incentive for achieving influence and maintain an ethical value for disciplined inquiry. Under the first environmental condition, the question is: What will the researcher do for the community with his or her power, trust, and support? Under this second condition, the question is: Will the research process be the vehicle for the researcher's desire for personal influence? Here the researcher will need to be vigilant to maintain difficult and quality work when there is social pressure to emerge as a true influential in the community.

THE SUPPORTIVE CONTEXT WHERE TRUST IS LOW, YET POWER IS HIGH: NO PROPHETS ALLOWED

This environmental condition will be troublesome for most academically oriented researchers. The option to be influenced is present in the community, but with expressions of doubt and suspicion about the benefits of research. The Biblical aphorism, "The prophet is not without honor, save in his own country," seems appropriate to describe this condition. The community is expected to test the community developer; persons will watch to see what the specialist studies, how committed he or she is to receiving input and advice from citizens, and how he or she responds to various community viewpoints. The challenge for the community developer is to make visible his or her competence, in spite of the supportive setting, and not make use of power until trust is achieved. With a consistent mode of responding to citizen requests for analyzing issues, the researcher can create positive conditions for trust. The preferred style under this condition is to create occasions where persons can directly participate in the entire research process, but particularly in the evaluation of research. If the community developer can respond to this challenge, he or she will learn much about the values of the community and be in a position for attributed power to be useful.

This environmental condition provides a very constructive challenge to expand the professional leadership of the community researcher. The presence of low trust for community research, under conditions of support and an option to influence, can be a stimulant for the research enterprise to become genuinely community based. As a result of working under this condition, the research process is expected to become responsive to the community, where the choice of research topics will be determined more and more by the needs and priorities of citizens. The research process is expected to expand under this condition of induced improvisation. The environmental condition provides a constructive set of experiences to communicate the legitimate role of divergnt methods of research for the training of future community developers. This environmental condition has the highest potential for learning how to adapt inquiry to community needs.

THE SUPPORTIVE CONTEXT WHERE BOTH TRUST AND POWER ARE LOW: HOW TO BE A WHITE ELEPHANT AND SURVIVE

This odd situation probably happens more often than we care to think about. Research *can* be tolerated as a symbol and as a form of conspicuous consumption. This environmental condition is expected to encourage research for the sake of research instead of research as organic to the community. This condition is probably the most tenuous for serious community-based inquiry, and it represents the greatest potential for the researcher to exploit the research process and to respond prematurely and unnecessarily to fads for the latest research technology. The community developer under this condition can be caught up with trying to "sell" the research process to the community. An easy adaptation is to do it through the display of techniques and hardware related to the research process. With the expected appeals of how the newest technology will help the research process, the community psychologist can succumb by demonstrating novelty in results in order to assure survival of the research process. These conditions breed a researcher who, like Willy Loman in *Death of a Salesman,* believes that one last big sale will bring salvation. This condition is expected to have the highest potential for alienating the investigator.

If the community developer can sustain such pressures for survival and deal openly to achieve trust and power, there is an opportunity for the research role to be catalytic for a new segment of the community. The community developer as researcher has to make the first move, however. This environmental condition can provide, by default, an opportunity for the community researcher to learn how to achieve creditability and initiate influence. In many ways this condition offers a setting for learning how to do good and useful research. But this condition requires a reserve of energy and personal commitment if the research investigator is to be acculturated. The researcher must relate to the diverse portions of the community and do research with the community to build a basis for trust and influence. There is an opportunity for the community developer to integrate the competencies for research technology with an analysis of community dynamics; as such it is a very apt condition for learning community research.

THE NONSUPPORTIVE CONTEXT WITH HIGH TRUST AND HIGH POWER: THE SHORT LIFE OF CHARISMA

Where there is little support, but where trust and power exist, the research process can have definite impact. The research investigator may even find conditions in this environment to be more constructive than in an environment where there is support. The pressures expected to be generated under conditions of nonsupport are for tangible results with high impact and influence. Such a setting can move the research investigator to select a topic and work hard to see that there is some benefit for the effort.

It is difficult, however, to do research that will encourage scientific activity to become a resource for the community when the community says "No." The absence of support for research creates an incentive to design an inquiry that can be carried out within a short period of time. Under this condition, the choice of the research problem becomes critical: to know the topics that will generate interest and impact over a brief period.

This particular condition can attract and appeal to investigators who enjoy a challenge of investing in research *and* investing in the community without being concerned about the tenure of the research operation. This condition offers incentive to plunge in, to try out ideas, to make a difference in the expression of the quality of life in the locale. This particular condition probably offers the best setting for immersion in the community. The returns can be many for the psychologist and for the community for a short, active, intense period of work to win support. This condition offers ample opportunity to learn how to achieve community commitment to continuous evaluation and for the community to value external criteria as hallmarks of truth. It is expected, more than any of the eight conditions, to provide an education in learning how to change community values. This condition is an excellent setting for the analysis of community life. As such, university training could not easily duplicate the opportunities for community study any more directly than does this condition of some trust and power without long-term support.

THE NONSUPPORTIVE CONTEXT WHERE TRUST IS HIGH, YET POWER IS LOW: MAKING IT AS A MARGINAL PERSON

In a community where the systematic investigation of topical issues and social problems is not valued and where people rely on their "folk wisdom" for coping and decision making, the research enterprise is defined outside the needed sphere of influence of their world. When there is trust in the research process, but when the likelihood of receiving long-term support and the mandate to influence is low, the research process is marginal. The research work is neither in nor out of the community; it is on the fringe of community values. The task for the research investigator under this condition is to create community support for research and to generate an interest in the community to take an active role to search out solutions for community problems. The research staff under this condition can work to build a source of support for the research organization and to test out the community's values for systematic inquiry. If the research staff selects topics that are genuine community issues, the very act of carrying out research can generate feedback to determine how much real influence the research enterprise is developing.

The processes of achieving influence and increasing the value for research *per se* are delicate ones and will require research investigators who are interested in an unyielding but focused effort to educate and promote under conditions where recognition is absent and where the faith of the community in the research staff is sparse. Such a condition can easily unwind motivations to participate in the research process. It is a sad but realistic finding that trust is not enough for substantial community work. Trust can allow the work to begin, but the prognosis for work is uncertain without a possibility of future influence. This condition requires ingenuity in responding both to the ambiguity of nonsupport and to the absence of accessibility to influence. This absence of support and influence in the presence of expectations of doing some good can be of help in the training of community research roles. The very constraint of marginality can be an unplanned and unwanted incentive to improvise, to try and do different studies to see what will work. The cost for the research process is that there will be less chance for the research skills to be well developed. Before really testing out an initial finding or developing a check on the validity of a theoretical interpretation, the need for survival will move the research on to new topics and new directions. Research under this condition is an "iffy" situation for the investigator and the community.

THE NONSUPPORTIVE CONTEXT WHERE TRUST IS LOW AND POWER IS HIGH: THE CRITIC'S PARADISE

This environmental condition encourages analysis and criticism as the most apt mode of operation and thereby sanctions an accepted role for research in our society. The condition exerts pressure on the community developer to maintain a high perch, to distribute the findings of research that charges the community to do something different. The role of researcher as critic devleops under this environmental condition, because the primary way the investigator does his or her work is to talk out loud. Without support, without a feeling from the community at large that research will lead somewhere, the investigator adopts a style to work for change through criticism. This particular environmental condition can help to turn an empirical research tradition into social philosophy. This is a difficult role to perform to achieve a constructive impact. The risk of the research process is that it grinds axes instead of clarifying issues for the community. The position of critic is enviable in some respects, since there is less need to worry about implementing findings. But the absence of trust can further insulate the criticism from the process of reality testing and identifying community needs. The research process under this condition can move to periodic, intellectual intrusions into the life of the community, with no commitment or desire on the part of the research staff to see how or if the criticism will culminate in anything useful. Certainly breaking the stereotype of research as a powerful pest is an option and a challenge.

The scientific training of the research staff may soon be forgotten under this condition or only referred to casually to lend dignity to carping. The absence in the community of an expectation of action reduces the pressure for producing explicit public statements based on disciplined inquiry. It is expected that a position of influence for

research, with nothing else, will limit the research performance and erode the commitment of the research staff to
relate to community needs. The critic's paradise is short-
lived.

THE NONSUPPORTIVE CONTEXT WHERE THERE IS NO TRUST AND NO POWER: COPING WITH A LOST CAUSE

Without support, trust, or power, what can happen? The
role of the research enterprise under these conditions is
lonely and monastic. Scenes from Samuel Beckett's *Krapps'
Last Tape* come to mind; there is little hope. There is little
hope for the development of social processes that insure
that empirical research will be useful for constructive community change. Certainly no one who wants to be useful,
who values action, or who enjoys seeing inquiry lead to
some change will select this condition as a preferred work
environment. All is not lost, however. While working under
these conditions, the researcher has a unique freedom to
see whether research techniques will work, if new research
strategies will have impact. This situation is deceptively
optimal as soil for the future development of the research
process and the research staff. As long as the staff can work,
try out ideas, and not succumb completely during the time
they are working, they can learn a great deal, not only about
the research process, but about their ability to respond to
stress and crisis conditions. There is something definitely
educational in learning under crisis conditions if one can
control the crisis or one's exit from the crisis environment.
For a short time this condition can be a genuine "hothouse" for developing competencies useful in both community research and personal survival.

The testing of research methods and styles of work
under such unresponsive conditions runs the risk, however, of burnout. The hothouse can scar! A planned recov-

ery period from this setting will be important before the investigator begins to prepare for the next research activity. What matters in working under this stress condition is not what happens to research or to the community, but what the research investigator makes of his or her experience before moving on to the next enterprise.

SUMMARY AND CONCLUSIONS

Community research is not a single act of scientific work applied in the same way to each community. These comments have affirmed that the research process varies from place to place, according to the qualities of community conditions. Examples of adaptive requirements for research derived from premises about eight environmental conditions representing two hypothetical levels of support, trust, and power have been presented. These ideas suggest that there is a need and opportunity for researchers who are community developers to consider research as a process related to community conditions. If communities vary, so goes the corollary, then research roles will vary.

These ideas are also based on the premise that the community developer values doing research that has impact. It has been proposed that there is pragmatic value for the community and the research staff to anticipate the outcomes of research. Working to achieve rapport with citizens and, at the same time, improving the range of influence are still important unknowns in community research. The challenge of understanding both processes is staggering and is a topic of much worth. Operational clarity for professional roles in community work is needed; attention to the research process in community work is long overdue.

BIBLIOGRAPHY AND REFERENCES

Campbell, D. T. Reforms as experiments. *American Psychologist,* 1969, **24,** 409–429.

Caplan, N., & Nelson, S. D. On being useful: The nature and consequences of psychological research on social problems. *American Psychologist,* 1973, **28,** 199–211.

Cottle, T. J. Show me a scientist who's helped poor folks and I'll kiss her hand. *Social Policy,* 1974, **4,** 33–37.

Kahn, R. L. Discussion. *Professional Psychology,* 1973, **4,** 237–245.

Kelman, H. C. The rights of the subject in social research: An analysis in terms of relative power and legitimacy. *American Psychologist,* 1972, **27,** 989–1016.

Smith, M. B. Is psychology relevant to new priorities? *American Psychologist,* 1973, **28,** 463–471.

Torres, Lorraine B. The participants in social science research. *Professional Psychology,* 1973, **4,** 211–216.

Vallance, T. R. Social science and social policy: Amoral methodology in a matrix of values. *American Psychologist,* 1972, **27,** 107–113.

AFTERWORD

Edward J. Blakely

What do we know now that we did not know before? How can we use what we now know? What difference does it make, anyway?

I suppose all books written and certainly all community development books are subject to these queries. In response to the first question, I believe that this book provides a convenient, even though incomplete, handle on the nebulous subject of community development research. It outlines what it is and gives some illustrations as to how it is done. Obviously a nice companion would be a series of selected research papers utilizing the methods discussed. If the demand is there, that need can be met. In fact, the *Journal of the Community Development Society* contains much of the best research of this kind.

Second, if you want to use the information contained in this book, there are many places to start. If you are an undergraduate student, you want to begin by testing the concepts discussed through a microcosmic research action project of some kind. If you are an advanced student or practitioner, you might want to develop your own paradigm. This book offers you many areas in which to operate. You may wish to use it, in other words, as a point of departure for your own theory building, concept testing, or even critical review of research in the community arena. If you are a teacher or researcher, you might use this book as a reference work or assigned reading. Although the book is not all-inclusive, it is a quick reference and shorthand way of giving others a statement as to what community development research is all about. Some academician may want to use it simply to describe to baffled colleagues, deans, and others the legitimacy of the community development research endeavor.

There is no answer to the last question. In many respects, you get what you are looking for. This book or others will not make the difference; only the reader can do that for himself or herself and for all those whom they attempt to help.

INDEX

220